SCHOOL TALK

GENDER AND ADOLESCENT CULTURE

Second paperback printing, 1997

Library of Congress Cataloging-in-Publication Data
Eder, Donna, 1951–
    School talk: gender and adolescent culture / by Donna Eder with
Catherine Colleen Evans and Stephen Parker.
        p.   cm.
    Includes bibliographical references and index.
    ISBN 0-8135-2178-5 (cloth : alk. paper)—
ISBN 0-8135-2179-3 (pbk. : alk. paper)
    1. Junior high school students—Social conditions.
2. Conversation analysis.   3. Junior high school students—
Attitudes.   4. Sex differences in education.   5. Adolescent
psychology.   I. Evans, Catherine Colleen, 1948–   .   II. Parker,
Stephen, 1955–   .   III. Title.
LC208.4.E33   1995
370.19'341—dc20   94-25220
                                                                           CIP

British Cataloguing-in-Publication information available

This research was initially supported by NIMH grant 36684.

To Natalie Eder,
whose courage in meeting the many challenges
of ALS (Lou Gehrig's disease)
is an inspiration for my writing
and for my life

Contents

Acknowledgments

This book would not have been possible without the assistance and support of many people. To begin with, I am grateful to the students and staff of Woodview who gave us this valuable opportunity of witnessing their school life on a daily basis over a three-year period. All of the research assistants on this project made extremely valuable contributions. Besides assisting in the collection of detailed, comprehensive data, Cathy Evans and Steve Parker went on to assist with the data analysis and writing of this book. I am particularly grateful to Cathy Evans for her insightful feedback throughout the study and for her substantial editing of the final manuscript. Stephanie Sanford also collected excellent data and helped to broaden the scope of the study. Janet Enke provided invaluable insights into the analysis of girls' talk and continued to engage in dialogues that were a constant source of inspiration as she went on to study the experience of older adoles-

ACKNOWLEDGMENTS

cents. David Kinney also followed many of these youths into their high school years, thereby expanding our understanding of adolescent school culture. Joyce Owens, Cindy Murphy, Angela Marato, Susan Moke, Mary Jean Burke, and Elizabeth Craft (who, sadly, did not live to see the book's completion) provided help with the detailed transcriptions and the preparation and coding of different types of data. Other graduate students, especially Melissa Milkie, Robin Simon, Lori Sudderth, Semya Hakim, and Beth Christianson, provided stimulating and helpful insights into the analysis of these data.

Many colleagues have read parts of this book and/or provided helpful feedback on earlier related papers. I am especially grateful to Patti Adler, Peter Adler, Bill Corsaro, Sue Fisher, David Heise, Nancy Lesko, Doug Maynard, and Brian Powell for giving generously of their time. I would also like to thank Gary Fine, Candy Goodwin, Chuck Goodwin, Linda Grant, Allen Grimshaw, Barbara Reskin, Deborah Tannen, and Barrie Thorne for their important comments at various stages in this project. I have also benefited greatly from the secretarial and computer assistance of Susan Duke, Eleanor Schloesser, Lorene Fox, and, especially, Chris Martindale.

This book would also not have been written without the support of family and friends over the years. I owe a great debt of gratitude to Natalie Eder (who also, sadly, did not live to see the book's completion) and Eugene Eder for their support of my academic efforts and curiosity since childhood. A special thanks to my sister, Joyce Feustel, for helping me "jargon-proof" the book. Also, I would like to thank Jim McDonough for encouraging me to write the initial grant and to undertake a project of this scope and Diane Felmlee for her support during the initial stages of this research. Discussions with Rima Merriman, Georg'ann Catalona, Peggy Cantrell, Tim Jackson, and other friends during the process of writing the book were also extremely helpful. I would like to especially thank Mark Blackwell for the many discussions we had that helped to frame the book in a way that conveys its broader social relevance.

I am also grateful to several young people who have taken the time to share their views on these issues and who have helped me identify what strategies can best help address some of the problems raised in this study. A special thanks to Caitlin Blackwell, Emmy Blackwell, Anna Beth Keim, Carolyn Kibbey, Bailey Eder, and Justin Anderson. Thanks also to Nissy Stetson and Shelly Miller for sharing insights based on their own experience in adolescence. Finally, I am grateful to my daughter, Megan, for her patience and for being a continual source of engaging humor and creativity.

SCHOOL TALK

1

Remember When?

Remember when you were a young teenager and just beginning to wonder where you fit into the ambiguous social world of junior high school? Remember when you sat down at a table in the lunchroom only to find you weren't welcome there? Remember when you wanted to avoid going to your locker and encountering yet another bully? Remember when you resorted to calling other people names to keep them from bugging you? Remember when fellow students were quick to let you know if your shirt wasn't the right name brand or tucked in the right way? Remember when even the comments of friends were sometimes difficult to understand—was that a friendly remark or was some type of insult implied?

Early adolescence is a time of great complexity and confusion. Suddenly, new social cliques are forming within the school setting. Because no one wants to be left out, there is often a strong desire to conform to the clothes, hairstyles, and even mannerisms of others. As one fourteen-year-old put it, "In most cases you have to abandon your individuality to fit in. You're trying to form yourself, but others are forming you." This is also often a time when the opposite sex is a complete mystery. Boys and girls tend to spend much of their free time apart, sitting at tables that become known as "the boys' table" and "the girls' table." One young man told my college class, "I always wondered what the girls in my school were talking about over there by themselves." Divisions such as this make young people aware of being male or female at a time when various forms of insecurity limit their willingness to explore a wider range of ways to express themselves.

Youth attempt to make sense of their perplexing new social world as they meet informally in school and in other settings. The everyday, taken-for-granted routines of friends during free-time lunch activities provide numerous opportunities to create shared meaning and a new sense of belonging. Many of these routines are based in language; informal talk becomes an important medium for creating mutual understanding. Frequently, students share stories about events in their lives, often starting them with the phrase, "Remember when . . ." Other forms of talk, such as gossip, teasing, and insulting, allow them to collectively create various notions of what it means to be male or female.

As adults, we can better understand current gender relations by reexamining that time in our own life span when they became increasingly significant. Most of us make the transition from childhood to adulthood within the world of public school. For this reason, our research team chose to observe adolescent development within this common setting. We set out to become "quiet friends" in lunchtime peer groups, hoping that by participating in these groups we could better appreciate their members' concerns and perspectives. Although we kept daily field notes and adopted low-profile roles, we allowed ourselves to be drawn into their social worlds. Noticing that we had arrived at lunch alone, some students initiated contact with us with polite, tentative questions. "Do you have someone to sit with?" they invited. "You can sit with us," others offered. From these beginnings, we soon were led to experiences that included hiding in hallways from teachers while a group of girls dragged a laughing boy into their bathroom and witnessing with other observers in back of the school building a first, daring kiss.

Many people with whom we have discussed our study have asked how we were able to immerse ourselves in something as painful as middle school life or even to walk once again inside a middle school building. One woman passionately remarked, "When I left junior high I closed the doors on that part of my life and have never looked back at it!" Admittedly, our own experiences during this study were sometimes quite uncomfortable, especially when we listened to unhappy confidences shared with us by young friends or felt compromised when confronted by sudden acts of cruelty. Times hadn't changed very much, we noted. As you read this book, you may experience, as we did, memories of your own junior high days—the awkwardness of not fitting in or of having people jealous of you because you fit in too well, the fear of witnessing your own body change and having others make fun of those changes because they found them intimidating, and the compromising of personal beliefs resulting from an overwhelming desire to be liked. Because of the pain and confusion many adults associate with this period of their own lives, they tend to forget that often bewildering transition. Although people reach some understanding during adolescence through their daily shared routines and concerns, other aspects remain a mystery, as confusing as when they first occurred. Consequently, we as adults are often less able than we would like to provide support and guidance to those currently in this important stage of life.

Four years after completing our study we invited some of the people we had videotaped as eighth-graders to watch themselves on tape. We had hoped to compare their perspectives on these interactions with our own. Instead, they were so surprised by their "childish" speech and behavior that we were unable to get beyond their cries of embarrassment. One girl exclaimed, " 'Cool your jets!'—I can't believe I really talked like that!" Given their reactions, it seems only fair, as we present their behavior in adolescence, to remind our readers that once upon a time we also participated in similar activities and used similar forms of speech. While the examination of early adolescent talk (theirs and ours) brings with it the risk of embarrassment, reopening a window into this unfamiliar yet powerful period of life also has many benefits.

The study upon which this book is based began with a broad inquiry into adolescent culture and language. Since our findings encompass too much information to be the topic of a single book, we will narrow our scope to one aspect of adolescent school culture that emerged as being particularly strong and important—the nature and construction of gender inequality. This discussion will build upon our greater understanding of various aspects of youth culture, such as social relations and speech activities.

Now that we have a clearer understanding of the nature of many types of daily speech routines among twelve- to fourteen-year-olds, it is important to understand how language becomes the basis for maintaining power differences between males and females as well as for providing creative opportunities to challenge limiting gender roles. In addition, a general knowledge of male and female school culture provides an important background for understanding the nature and construction of sexuality and gender relations.

Given the increasingly dangerous climate that females face in this country, a greater understanding of gender inequality is essential. Public focus has increasingly turned to widespread sexual harassment not only in the workplace but also within our public schools. These incidents are not limited to harassment by those with greater power and status within the institution, but include harassment by male peers as well. Sexual abuse by peers is also reflected in the pervasiveness of date and acquaintance rape. Although the findings of different studies vary depending on the questions asked, it now appears that as many as one-fourth of all young women will have unwanted intercourse, and over three-fourths of them will encounter some type of sexual aggression. Given the seriousness of these social problems, important questions arise regarding the strong link between power abuse and sexuality. Specifically, why have sexual relations become an arena for competition and conquest leading to insensitive behavior on the part of so many males?

Equally disturbing are the cultural beliefs surrounding this climate of male sexual aggression. In the much publicized case of the Spur Posse Gang, the high school athletes from Lakewood, California, who openly bragged about their success at having had intercourse with as many as sixty girls, most of the initial charges of rape, unlawful intercourse, and lewd conduct were dropped. Many parents and community members defended these boys, claiming that they were simply "victims of their male hormones," while others argued that their behavior represented "typical masculine behavior." Some parents even turned the blame on the girls who were the actual victims of their sons' sexual aggression, referring to them as "sluts." Since it is highly unlikely that these girls had nearly as many sexual encounters as the boys involved, and, given the ages of some of the girls (as young as eleven and twelve), this case vividly reveals the existence of a continued double standard regarding sexuality. While it is normative for boys to have strong and perhaps "uncontrollable" sexual desires, any girl who has sex, even as a victim of rape, may be labeled a slut.

A second nationally discussed case reveals how the most vulnerable girls are often the targets of sexual abuse. This case, which took place in the affluent suburb of Glen Ridge, New Jersey, involved a mentally retarded teenager who was persuaded to join a group of popular male athletes with the promise of getting a date with one of them. In the end, seven of these boys stayed on, pressing her to masturbate and perform oral sex before some of them raped her with various objects. Again the attorneys of the accused males argued that "boys will be boys—pranksters, foolarounds." They also portrayed the victim as a seductive "Lolita" who aggressively pursued men, making these young men and their raging hormones vulnerable to her instead of she being vulnerable to them. The jury sided with the prosecution, who claimed that the young woman was not mentally competent to consent to these sexual acts (her IQ was 64 and her social skills at the level of an eight-year-old).

The cultural beliefs presented by these defense attorneys and offered by parents in behalf of the Spur Posse Gang reflect the entrenched, taken-for-granted nature of sexual inequality. They show the importance of examining the ways in which aggressive behavior is systematically promoted by organized sports in public schools as well as through the daily speech routines of adolescent boys. We hope the findings of this study will call to question the biological and/or "normative" labeling of such behavior and show the serious social problem that it has become.

At the same time, we consider it important to examine factors that contribute to gender inequality within female peer culture. For example, a focus on being attractive is currently promoted through school activities such as cheerleading and through girls' gossip and other daily speech routines. Do contemporary practices prepare adolescent girls to deal with the competitive, aggressive sexual style promoted in male culture? Or do they further undermine the possibility of equality in sexual relations by focusing on female appearance?

The next chapter places this study in a theoretical framework that includes both an interpretive and a dialectic approach to the study of gender, talk, and inequality. In it, we will examine previous research on peer culture in school settings and show the importance of looking at both institutional and language practices in order to understand better the nature of gender inequality within public schools. Since this chapter includes sociological concepts and terms that may not be familiar to nonsociologists, some readers may wish to go directly to chapter three.

2

Gender,
Talk, and School Culture

If we are to be successful in promoting social change, we need to understand how daily practices in schoools and other institutions affect the construction of beliefs about gender definitions and gender inequality. We believe that a better understanding of practices that currently generate inequality can lead to different practices and the creation of a more egalitarian consciousness.[1] Our study draws upon two theoretical frameworks for understanding daily practices—the interpretive approach to the construction of peer culture and the dialectic approach to the study of power and discourse.

The interpretive approach to the construction of culture emphasizes the collective, public nature of developing cultural meanings. The basic argument is that people construct their social worlds through interaction with others.[2] Children as well as adults are viewed as being capable of actively constructing their own shared understandings. This means that they do not simply conform to the gender roles and norms of adults, but instead often comment on or challenge them while engaged in their own active construction of gender.

Within this framework there has been increaased attention to the importance of cultural routines. Because routines, such as greetings, insult exchanges, and gossip, are recurrent and predictable activities, they provide people with a sense of belonging to a group with shared understandings.[3] The predictable, underlying structure of these routines provides opportunities for displaying and creating cultural knowledge.[4]

The interpretive model sees children's cultural knowledge as both reflecting the beliefs of the adult world and containing unique interpretations and aspects of the children's own peer culture. This knowledge is often described as having both reproductive and productive aspects.[5] Routines and rituals convey a sense of taken-for-granted knowledge, thereby reproducing traditional gender ideas, but they can also be a vehicle for challenging traditional gender messages.[6]

Research by William Corsaro on American and Italian nursery school children has shown the importance of daily routines.[7] Predictable patterns of interaction are established through "approach-avoidance" games in which children alternate between approaching a threatening person or group and then running away and through common speech routines such as insult exchanges and the Italian version of ritual conflict, *discussione*. The predictable nature of these routines not only allows young children to participate readily in conversations with their peers but also provides a structured framework that can be embellished with creative adaptations.

Marjorie Goodwin studied a wider range of speech activities, including insult exchanges, storytelling, dramatic role-play, and gossip, used by black, urban youth to demonstrate cultural knowledge. She found that both boys and girls used a wide range of speech routines and that different routines were used in different situations. For example, girls seldom made direct requests when working on a shared task, but such requests were a common feature of their dramatic role-play. Goodwin's work is also instrumental in showing how language is used to shape social alignments and social identities, thereby creating patterns of social organization, not just reflecting them.[8]

Another interpretive orientation has been to analyze gender differences in language from an anthropological perspective. Here the emphasis has been on examining the development of different subcultures in which language is used and interpreted in quite different ways.[9] Deborah Tannen has shown how some misunderstandings between men and women stem from lack of awareness of the opposite gender's norms and styles of discourse. To the extent that these misunderstandings promote negative stereotypes of the other gender they serve to enhance male-female conflict. These misunderstandings can also promote gender inequality, with women often being perceived as being too emotional, insecure, unassertive, and so on from the perspective of male culture.

This line of research has its limitations, however, in that it can imply greater gender uniformity than actually exists. Although there are clearly gender differences in talk, these differences may be exaggerated by such studies.[10] Instead of emphasizing gender differences, Robert Connell has advocated a focus on gender practices, which allows for a greater understanding of the complex and dynamic ways in which gender influences people's lives.[11] Such a focus provides the opportunity to study processes of social change as well as processes of social reproduction.

Although research that emphasizes equal but different styles is meant to counteract the view that a male style is superior, this approach can be misleading. Taken on its own, it implies greater neutrality in gender and culture than actually exists. Given the power differences between men and women in contemporary American society, this avenue of inquiry cannot fully address problems of gender inequality. For example, women who adopt male styles of touch and posture are not necessarily viewed as having successfully assimilated to a different culture; rather, they are often perceived in other terms, such as being more sexually available or promiscuous.[12] Likewise, girls who insult boys as a means of responding to or warding off their insults are sometimes negatively labeled as "sluts" or "bitches."[13]

In this study we examine a range of formal and informal practices within the school setting in order to understand how gender inequality is constructed. We give particular attention to the key role of speech routines during informal talk. We focus on the four most common interactive speech routines used by early adolescents—insulting, teasing, collaborative storytelling, and gossip. We examine how the structure of these various routines constrains adolescents' ability to challenge traditional gender beliefs, while at the same time daily reinforcing those very beliefs. We also consider the extent to which certain routines offer flexibility for more spontaneous expressions, which, in many cases, include mocking or resisting traditional cultural beliefs.

The other key theoretical framework is one that directly unites issues of power and discourse. This approach attempts to understand the interrelated nature of language, belief systems, and social relations, especially unequal social relations. There has been an awareness for some time of the important role of belief systems in maintaining inequality, but only recently have people begun to examine the crucial role language plays in this process.[14] On the one hand, language reflects a type of power that limits and constrains modes of expression and beliefs. Generally, discourse in formal settings and institutions is highly constricting, but all forms of talk involve some degree of constraint.[15] In fact, the very predictability of the routines discussed earlier is based on their underlying rules, which constrain the kinds of ideas that can be expressed.

Related to this, language is also a key process for promoting existing forms of inequality by constraining the expression of different cultural beliefs. For example, the double standard that normalizes active sexuality in men while making it deviant for women is in part maintained by the language we speak. As Dale Spender notes, there are 220 words for sexually promiscuous women but only 20 words for sexually promiscuous men.[16] Sue Lees found that girls are labeled "slags" and "sluts" for many forms of independent behavior, such as going places on their own and talking aggressively to boys who insult them, as well as for having multiple sexual partners.[17] Thus, current language practices control many aspects of women's behavior as well as their sexual conduct.

However, language also reflects another type of power—the power to create and shape reality. Here language is seen as an active process, and perhaps the most vital aspect of social relations because it "sets up the positions that allow social interactions to occur."[18] In this sense, discourse, whether written or oral, has the potential to create new knowledge, new beliefs, and a new consciousness. It reflects the ability of language to create thought, rather than simply be constrained by current belief systems or underlying discourse rules. It is not surprising that many oppressed people talk about the critical role of creative expression—such as fiction, poetry, or music—for surviving under systems of domination.[19] Language is often the only means available for constructing a different reality that goes beyond current beliefs systems and social relations that reinforce domination.

This perspective shows the essential nature of language as both a process for maintaining cultural beliefs of inequality and a process for challenging those beliefs. As Alexandra Todd and Sue Fisher note, an understanding of language allows us more fully to comprehend the construction of consciousness.[20] To the extent we are aware of the nature of certain daily speech routines, the better we can see the underlying beliefs behind them. These beliefs can then be examined to see if they reflect the type of social relations we desire to have in our society. Both new ways of thinking and new modes of discourse will ultimately be needed to establish different social relations, along with changes in practices at the institutional level (in this case, changes in school policy). While language is crucial to a greater awareness of both beliefs and social relations, change in use of speech is only one aspect of an interrelated set of processes that must occur in order for meaningful change to come about.[21]

Research in School Settings

Because most youths share this common opportunity to come together with their peers, school settings have been important sites for the study of peer culture. Adult beliefs appear to have a stronger impact on peer culture there than elsewhere, so school settings provide an important arena in which to study the construction of gender inequality. Helena Wulff found that school peer culture is more strongly influenced by adult beliefs than peer cultures in homes, in youth centers, or on street corners, perhaps because it occurs within the context of formal activities (both academic and extracurricular) that are led by adults.[22] School settings also tend to promote a high degree of gender segregation, in part because student activities such as chasing games, romantic teasing, and "cooties" labeling reinforce the boundaries between boys and girls during informal play.[23] These informal activities, along with teacher and school traditions such as having girls and boys line up separately or engage in informal contests, result in minimal interaction between girls and boys during school time.[24] In contrast, Marjorie Goodwin found much less gender segregation and more flexibility in the number and type of daily routines in her study of neighborhood peer culture among black, urban youth.[25]

Studies of peer cultures within American schools reveal a strong concern with status and social hierarchy. James Coleman, in his classic research on adolescent concerns in ten midwestern schools, reports being shocked by the pervasive concern among adolescents with popularity as opposed to academic success.[26] This preoccupation may be partly due to the strong role that extracurricular activities have historically played in American schools. Cross-cultural research has shown that students in Danish high schools, which do not have extracurricular programs, are much less concerned with popularity and less aware of the existence of leading crowds than are students in American schools.[27]

Many studies have found a strong link between participation in extracurricular activities and peer status.[28] The central factor appears to be the greater visibility provided students who participate in key extracurricular activities such as male athletics, cheerleading, and drama, since visibility is essential to being known by the large number of students in most middle schools and high schools.[29] In addition to visibility, extracurricular activities provide other resources, such as special privileges and greater control of time and space.[30] These privileges typically benefit white and middle-class students who are most likely to participate in high-profile activities, but in some urban, lower-class schools, black students have been found to be more involved than white students in school life through their greater participation in athletic activities.[31]

Middle schools and junior high schools are of particular interest because they have the most unidimensional status hierarchies.[32] Research has found that there are fewer extracurricular activities available per student in middle school than in either the equivalent upper grades of elementary schools or in high schools.[33] David Kinney found that this presents a situation in which students perceive that they have limited opportunities to gain recognition from their peers, leading many to feel like social failures during this critical time in adolescence.[34] By high school, students have more opportunities to join activities, and they often downplay the existence of cliques and rankings.[35] The powerful influence of school environment is also evident in research by Roberta Simmons and Dale Blyth, which shows that students who attend junior high schools in seventh grade have much lower self-esteem throughout junior high and high school than do students who remain in elementary schools for seventh and eighth grade. [36]

Studies of peer culture have also found that school environments involve a high degree of gender segregation during lunch and recess, with the highest degree occurring during the middle-school years. [37] As early as elementary school, male and female peer cultures have distinctive concerns and factors that influence peer status. [38] For example, girls were found to gain status through family background, appearance, and having more freedom at home, while boys gained status through athletic ability, being cool, and being tough. [39]

Many studies of high school peer culture have focused on working-class students. Although these studies do not link gender issues with peer status, they do show that boys and girls often resist mainstream culture by embracing very different concerns. For example, although Paul Willis found that fighting and defiance of rules were central for white working-class boys, other studies have found that marriage and romance are important for white working-class girls, and fashion and beauty are important for both white and black girls. [40]

While issues of power and resistance have generally been examined in regard to social class, one large study of social class reproduction in Australian secondary schools included an examination of gender reproduction. Robert Connell and his colleagues found that masculinity and femininity took on multiple forms within a single school, with one form being predominant and most valued. They also found that gender regimes can change over time as different school practices shift. Specifically, some schools were starting to emphasize girls' academic success, while other schools continued to reward their social success. [41]

There were no apparent similar changes in school practices aimed at masculinity. Even in upper-class schools, the predominant form of masculinity focused on aggressiveness and stemmed largely from participation in male athletics. Football was explicitly intended to develop masculinity by using physical strength to demonstrate and test one's superiority over others. Although not all boys participated in football or conformed to this type of masculinity, even those who did not had to come to terms with this dominating form of masculinity, which defined them as "losers" despite success in other areas.

This research was among the first to draw attention to the construction of masculinity as a dominating and potentially sexist practice that results in the subordination of other boys as well as of girls. In another study of sexism and classism, Joyce Canaan found that high-status boys established dominance primarily in regard to low-status, often overweight, boys whom they verbally insulted and physically harassed. Since girls were viewed as only marginally interesting, they were not the primary targets of the boys' aggressive acts.[42]

Most research has not focused on beliefs about male-female relationships and their critical role in gender inequality. Barrie Thorne is among the few who have begun to explore this important topic, finding that as early as elementary school, boys are using sexual insults and approaching male-female relations in a daring, aggressive manner.[43] Girls, on the other hand, value intimacy and emotional disclosure as they develop a very different view of male-female relations and relationships in general. By high school, Sue Lees finds that girls are controlled by a double standard that defines active male sexually as normal and active female sexuality as deviant. This control occurs through negative labels such as "slut" and "slag," which define girls primarily by their sexual reputation and are widely used to prevent girls from engaging in a range of independent behaviors as well as from having an active sense of their own sexuality.[44]

Occasionally, perceptions of girls are discussed in studies of male peer culture. For example, in a study of young boys in the context of baseball team membership, Gary Fine mentions that girls were discussed as objects of sexual conquest as boys talked about "how far they got."[45] Likewise, Paul Willis reports that girls were viewed as sexual objects and as being weak, indirect, and sexually passive.[46] In these studies, male perceptions were noted but not examined in terms of sexual inequality, reflecting a general tendency in much social research to associate power with issues of social class, but not with gender.

The Construction of Gender Inequality

This book examines two type of gender-related practices—institutional and language-based—within a school setting. The school environment is an ideal setting in which to study gender issues because it reveals the ways in which insecurities created by the social-status hierarchies of public schools make gender processes more powerful. The school context is further affected by the social-class and racial composition of students which set up other interrelated forms of status dynamics. In line with previous studies that have found that gender messages are often conveyed outside the classroom, we focus on extracurricular activities that explicitly convey messages regarding masculinity and femininity—male athletics and cheerleading. At the same time, we believe that the daily language practices of students themselves are central for understanding how people create their own gender meanings. Most of this book is therefore devoted to an in-depth examination of students' informal talk. Given the powerful nature of gender messages and the lack of flexibility in certain language routines, we show how girls as well as boys routinely engage in the construction of gender inequality. We also show, however, that many adolescents do not fully conform to these relatively powerful messages. Instead, many girls and some boys are able to challenge certain messages by using more flexible language routines such as story-telling and teasing.

While the gender practices and messages that contributed to gender inequality in this school reflect the most common concerns in their respective female and male peer cultures, they are not practices in which *all* students participated.[47] Also, because we focus on gender practices, it is inevitable that differences in the experiences of boys and girls are highlighted. Therefore, we believe it is important to draw attention to some striking similarities in the daily language activities of both genders. For example, despite the stereotypical idea that only girls gossip, we found that boys also frequently discussed and evaluated students who were not present at this time. Some of the girls in the school frequently participated in ritual insulting, an activity that has been associated in the past with boys and with Afro-Americans.[48] Both boys and girls often engaged in collaborative forms of talk, especially collaborative storytelling. In fact, boys were primarily interested in narratives about peer group activities that several boys could tell jointly, defying the stereotype that boys only engage in conflictual and independent modes of talk.

In addition, boys and girls in this school shared many concerns, such as being accepted and recognized by their peers. They were equally concerned with having a sense of belonging within their peer groups and used a variety of strategies to enhance group solidarity. For example, girls used collaborative teasing to reduce conflict stemming from jealousy toward other group members.[49] Boys modified the rules of informal athletic games to reduce conflict stemming from differences in their athletic skills.[50]

While this book focuses on a particular age level, that is, early adolescence, we see the gender practices that people are exposed to in this period as part of a larger set of reciprocal processes across age levels. Younger children draw on adolescent and adult notions of gender, while adolescents bring aspects of childhood culture with them as they develop new shared meanings. At any age level, new gender meanings may be created through collective practices.

Research at the elementary level shows that concerns that previously were believed to belong to the adolescent realm are now showing up in childhood, along with certain forms of gender inequality.[51] At the same time, studies of high school and college students reveal a continual emphasis on aggressiveness for men and attractiveness for women, at least in certain school contexts.[52] At each age level, certain practices contribute to maintaining these traditional gender interests. Thus, while we do not view the particular practices examined here as being the initial or single influence on adolescents' gender meanings, we do see them as being active contributors in this ongoing reciprocal process. Since most previous research has centered around gender construction at the elementary or high school level, this book fills an important gap in our understanding of gender practices in schools by focusing on the critical middle school years.

3

Entering the World of Middle School

Woodview School, the setting for this study, is located on the outskirts of a medium-sized midwestern community. Many students eagerly look forward to their lunchtime break, when they can socialize with their friends. The lunchroom itself becomes transformed from a quiet lineup of empty tables and chairs to a lively and sometimes rowdy setting, as students scramble to be first in lunch line and to save seats around tables for friends who will arrive later. The only adults to be seen among the masses of young active bodies are the food workers behind the counters and cash registers, one or two custodians, and the school principal. Unlike the classrooms from which the students have just arrived, the lunchroom environment bears the clear mark of adolescent peer culture.

When I decided to study the social experiences and conversations of adolescents in a middle school setting, I looked for a school that would be typical of other schools in the Midwest. I avoided schools that had a large number of students from academic or wealthy backgrounds and instead chose one that had a range of students from middle- to lower-class backgrounds. The students at the school were predominantly Euro-American; they came from rural homes as well as urban ones. The school itself offered a limited number of extracurricular activities for students during and after school. Both girls and boys could choose four different athletic activities, one for each eight-week session. They could also participate in a range of music activities, both instrumental and choral. In addition, girls could try out for the cheerleading squad. This range of extracurricular activities is typical of middle schools in the Midwest.

Once I had permission from the school board and principal to do the study, I minimized my association with adults, deciding that if I wanted to study the culture of adolescents I needed to participate in it on their terms. So I (and the research assistants who later joined me) entered the lunchroom without any introductions from adults. Several teachers, assuming I was a substitute teacher, kindly showed me where the teachers ate lunch during the first week or two. This reminded me again of how much the lunchroom represented student, not adult, territory.

As any new student at school knows, it can be rather painful to go through the process of becoming accepted by other students. Similarly, we all reported our own feelings of discomfort in early field notes as we wondered if any students would join us at lunch or appear friendly enough for us to feel comfortable joining them. Since I was also observing extracurricular activities, I started joining groups based on my associations with students in those activities. For example, I was easily able to join a seventh-grade group through a girl I met at volleyball practice. In eighth grade I did not feel comfortable joining any of the groups, which all seemed to be relatively closed to newcomers. For several weeks I only attended the sixth- and seventh-grade lunch periods.[1] When I did return to the eighth-grade lunch I again sat by myself. This time, however, a girl I knew from volleyball practice came up and said, "What are you doing sitting by yourself! Come over and join me." Later I realized that most of the eighth-grade groups had clearly defined members; the only people who did not have friends to sit with at lunch were the few highly visible isolates. This helped to explain my intense discomfort about sitting alone in eighth grade, as well as this student's desire to "save" me from the potential disaster of social isolation. The group I was invited to join was the highest-status group in eighth grade. Once I was associated with this group it was easy to join other groups, and at midyear I switched to a different eighth-grade group based on some new friendships with gymnastic team members.

Because I had ended up joining groups that sat on the high-status side of the cafeteria, the first research assistant to join the study, Stephanie Sanford, joined four different groups on the lower-status side. Her previous research at a local Girls Club provided her with some natural connections with two groups of girls. In the second year of the study, Cathy Evans replaced Stephanie as a research assistant and joined some of the same groups. She also joined the lowest-status group in the school, consisting predominantly of special education students. This meant that we now had information about girls at every social level within this school. Between Cathy and myself we were able to follow two seventh-grade groups into their eighth-grade year and one group from sixth to eighth grade. In the third year of the study, Steve Parker began to collect data on all-male groups. Since he was observing extracurricular activities at the school he was able to join three groups on the high-status side of the cafeteria through his associations with male athletes. He joined two other groups from the low-status side, one through an association with some football players and one through an initial association with a team manager. Altogether, we were able to observe a total of fifteen different groups—nine female, five male, and one mixed-gender group.

When we met students we introduced ourselves by telling them we were from Indiana University, or simply "from IU," and that we were interested in doing a study to find out what they liked to talk about and what their interests were. I told them that I would be coming to lunch on a regular basis and that someday I might write a book about what I found out. Most students were somewhat flattered that we had chosen their school to study, and many were excited by the idea of a book. Some students, however, never quite understood why we were so interested in their lives. Halfway through the first year one eighth-grader turned to me and said, "I still don't understand why you come to eat lunch with us when you could be eating lunch with college boys."

We were not asked by the principal to supervise the students in any way, which left us free to relate to them as older friends. Most of the time we adopted a "quiet friend" role, participating in conversations and routines only to the degree necessary for acceptance as part of the group. Certain routines, like insulting, demanded the ability to respond appropriately, and Steve, who encountered more of this in his interaction with the boys, found ways to respond to the insults he received, which further strengthened his rapport. Other groups had a rowdier style of interacting, sometimes requiring more physical play on the part of the researcher. All of us witnessed examples of swearing fairly early on. Swearing apparently was against school rules; when we ignored it, students realized that we were not going to report rule violations to anyone, and we quickly developed a greater level of rapport. They would tell their friends not to worry if they swore in front of us, or simply passed the word around that we were "okay."

It may be that the people we sat with did alter their behavior somewhat because of our presence. This was less and less likely to be the case as the months went on, since they tended to be quite spontaneous in their free-time behavior and would not have wanted to constrain it over a long period. In particular, activities such as insulting, gossip, teasing, and storytelling were so routine that it is unlikely that they were modified greatly for our benefit. (For more information about the methods used for this study, see the appendix.)

Seating Patterns in the Lunchroom

After we had attended lunch for a short time, it became clear to us that considerable differences existed in social relationships across the three grades. In the sixth grade there were few stable groups and no groups that appeared to have more status than others. In the seventh grade the groups were more stable, and a hierarchy was beginning to emerge. By eighth grade there was a clearly defined social ranking of relatively stable cliques.

The existence of defined groups was sometimes explicitly referred to by students, who would make comments such as, "This isn't your group," or "Your group's outside." However, the main way in which groups became defined was through seating arrangements at lunch. During the first year of the study, the three grades had separate lunch periods. In the second year, one lunch period was dropped, so students from different grades ate lunch together. Some students began sitting with groups at different grade levels, but most continued to sit with students in their own grade.[2] Students could sit wherever they wanted during their lunch period, and they went to considerable effort to ensure that they sat with friends and preferred acquaintances if at all possible. This was accomplished primarily by saving seats. This strategy was also used to prevent other students from sitting with a group. If someone the group didn't want to be associated with or didn't like approached an empty seat at the table, she or he was often told the seat was being saved for someone else.

Sixth-graders had the most flexible seating patterns during lunch. Few groups sat together regularly throughout the year, and most students sat with different groups on different days. Because seating arrangements were continually negotiated, we saw open attempts to include and exclude certain students. In the following example from our field notes, Penny[3] was excluded from a group with whom she had previously sat:

> Some visitors were sitting at their table, so they were trying to save the remaining seats for their friends. The main conflict arose when Penny sat in one of those seats and they told her all of them were saved. She looked a little dejected that they weren't going to let her sit with them. Then she looked around and said, "Well, where's Pam's group," and went over and talked to them. [Donna's notes]

There were no clear top groups throughout sixth grade for boys and during most of the year for girls. After cheerleading tryouts in May, however, some of the newly selected cheerleaders and their friends began to sit together occasionally. After the new cheerleaders did some routines for a pep session in the spring, they made a conscious attempt to all sit together at lunch:

> I noticed that Jane had saved a place on either side of her. Some girls were asking if they could sit there, and she was telling them that they were reserved for the cheerleaders. However, Betty's [a new cheerleader] two friends were sitting with the group even though they weren't cheerleaders. Judy noticed this and told Doreen that she and Peggy had asked to sit with them and they said no, it was just the cheerleaders, but that now they had let Betty's friends sit there. [Donna's notes]

Seating patterns among seventh-graders were more stable; many students sat with the same group for months at a time. By this time, a social ranking of groups had developed. The highest-status group among the boys consisted entirely of boys involved in football, wrestling, and/or basketball. For girls, it consisted of most or all the cheerleaders and many of the student council members. Another status division in seating arrangements developed in this grade. Both of these high-status groups, along with several other higher-status groups (including other athletes and/or student council members), sat on one side of the cafeteria. These students often wore name-brand clothes, and many of them appeared to be from middle-class and upper-working-class backgrounds. The students on the other side of the cafeteria appeared, from their dress, to be primarily from lower-working-class backgrounds. (Social class will be used throughout to refer not only to the income level of the students' families but also to the students' sense of others' degree of refinement. This typically includes the occupation and education level of parents, but can also include styles of dress, speech, and behavior related to an urban versus rural lifestyle, as it does in the case of this community and school.)

By eighth grade, the seating arrangements were very stable; most students sat with the same group for the entire year. During the first year, the high-status boys and girls sat together in one large mixed-sex group, which included all eight cheerleaders and many of the male athletes. The social-class division in seating patterns was also more apparent in eighth grade. Only a few students from middle-class backgrounds sat on the side of the cafeteria with the less popular students.

The extracurricular activities that most strongly influenced seating patterns were cheerleading and male sports. Although girls also participated in sports, they generally did not sit with their team members at lunch. Nor did band, orchestra, or jazz members usually sit together. A number of girls in one group happened to participate in chorus, but they explained that their friendships stemmed from being together in elementary school.

Although there was some curriculum tracking in this middle school, it did not appear to have a strong effect on students' friendships; we had no idea which students in the school were the highest academic achievers until the honor roll was announced at the end of the year. Some of the special education students sat together at lunch, however, in part because they were placed in separate classrooms at the time of the study, which made it difficult for them to form other friendships.

The Groups That Were Studied

The fifteen groups we studied ranged in size from two to twenty-one members.[4] The two high-status groups were the largest—the eighth-grade elite group consisted of twelve girls and nine boys, and the seventh-grade elite group consisted of thirteen boys. The five medium-high-status groups ranged in size from two to nine members. The seven medium-low-status groups ranged in size from four to twelve members, with the largest group being a rather diffuse group of sixth-grade students. The low-status group consisted of six regular members.[5] In choosing the number of groups at each status level we tried to represent the student population we were studying. Since most students were in medium-high and medium-low status groups, most of the groups we observed represented these middle rankings. Previous studies of school settings have often focused on a more limited number of groups and sometimes present a biased view of school life by only studying the high-status groups.[6]

In order to provide a sense of the group dynamics at different status levels, we will describe some of the male and female groups at each level. Hank, Mike, Eric, and their friends belonged to the most visible and highest-status male group. Every member participated in at least two school-sponsored sports.

Five members of this group went with cheerleaders during the school year. Hank and his friends understood that they were viewed as preps (high-school students who wear name-brand clothes) and, like other preps, had a basic acceptance of the school's official values and goals. At the same time, they saw themselves as superior to other prep groups—tougher, more defiant, and more popular with females. Lunchroom interactions in this group were characterized by high levels of aggressiveness and a willingness to challenge others.[7]

The medium-high-status male groups that were studied also consisted of athletes; they at times intermixed with boys in the highest-status group. The leader of one of these groups was Bobby. Bobby possessed exceptional verbal skills, was a very good basketball player, and was well liked by popular girls. Members of this group saw themselves as preps, but accepted the fact that Hank's group ranked higher in the social ranking of the school than they did. They admired the toughness and defiance exhibited by Hank's group and were envious of the confidence displayed in their interactions with females. Interactional routines within this group were quite distinct from those found in Hank's group. There was more storytelling and more self-parody, and much less insulting and direct challenging. This was largely a function of Bobby's presentational style and talents. Others participated in these routines, but they clearly depended on him to be the primary performer.

The medium-low groups were not as cohesive as the other male groups. One group centered around Walter, the manager of the football team. He ate lunch with his best friend, Jeff, every day; six other boys joined them on a regular basis. Many of these boys had little in common and tended to direct their comments and attention at Walter. Jeff was the only one to participate in a school-sponsored sport. At least four of the boys in this group were in advance-track classes, which was surprising, because academic achievements or interests were never discussed during lunch. Interaction in this group was characterized by telling jokes, reenacting movie scenarios and comedy routines, and humor based on bodily functions and the violation of socially acceptable behavior.

Girls' groups at the medium-high level were often based on earlier friendships. In one group, some girls also had school activities in common, such as gymnastics and choir. Penny, Bonnie, and many of the other girls in this group were very interested in popularity and wanted to be more popular. Only a few girls in this group went with boys. Instead of talking about boys, they talked about other girls' appearance and behavior; this talk often took the form of gossip. Members also enjoyed telling humorous stories about shared experiences in choir or study hall.

The medium-low-status girls' groups were generally louder and more exuberant in their behavior. Natalie, Ellen, and Gwen formed the center core of one of these groups and were all mutual best friends. They and the other girls in this group participated in a wide range of different speech activities on a regular basis, including insulting as well as teasing, gossip, and storytelling. Although this group sat on the low-status side of the cafeteria, they had relatively high status among students on that side. These girls enjoyed the opportunity to let go and freely express themselves during their free time with friends. Several of them were physically active in the lunchroom or media center, often jumping out of their chairs to chase around after someone. Most of the girls in this group were interested in boys, and two boys became temporary members of their group, sitting with it for short periods during the year.

Carol, Wanda, and the other girls in the lowest-status group were not as physically active as the girls in Natalie's group. Most of these girls knew each other through special education classes, although other girls who had trouble finding groups to join became regular or temporary members of this group. These girls seldom participated in the speech activities (such as teasing, gossip, and storytelling) that were common in other girls' groups, although some of them would insult students outside the group.

They were more likely to share information or have other types of brief conversations. The failure to participate in more varied speech routines may have been due the wide range of communication skills among the girls in this group.

Boy-Girl Interaction

Although most of the groups we studied (as well as most groups in the school) were solely or predominantly same-gender groups, considerable boy-girl interaction took place at all grade levels. These interactions can be grouped into three main patterns. The eighth-grade high-status group had both male and female members. The predominant pattern within this group was for couples to "go together" for relatively long periods—several months at a time. Other couples "went together" for shorter periods, however, and some group members did not have a regular girlfriend or boyfriend.

Another pattern was for a boy to sit with a girls' group for a shorter time or vice versa. Usually this person was either currently "going with" one of the group members, had previously gone with one of them, or was interested in going with someone in the group. Occasionally, a younger or smaller boy would sit with a group of girls, and, while romantic teasing often was aimed at him, it did not necessarily result in a romantic relationship.

Still another pattern was to have boys stop by and talk briefly with an all-girl group (or girls with an all-boy group.) These might be students group members currently liked or were "going with." In other cases, they were friends of people who liked someone in the group, serving as contacts to help initiate or mediate romantic relationships between students. This pattern was most common in seventh-grade groups.

The term *going together* was widely used to describe a variety of male-female relationships.[8] In some cases the couples spent a lot of time together at school and relationships were relatively long-term, lasting several months. This was quite rare, however, and group members were impressed by relationships that lasted as long as three weeks, considering that a very long time to be going with someone. Most relationships were quite brief, lasting from one day to two weeks. Some involved minimal or no contact between the couple, who had simply informed their close friends that they were willing to go with each other, leaving it to friends to initiate the relationship on their behalf. In one case, when asked the last name of his girlfriend, a boy replied, "I don't know, but I'm going to find out." This comment captures the relatively nonserious nature of many of these involvements. At the same time, despite their typical brevity, some breakups involved strong emotions in both girls and boys. These emotions were expressed, especially by girls, as intense sadness at the time of the breakup and later as strong jealousies centered on the new romantic partners of their former boyfriends.

4

Segregating the Unpopular from the Popular

The students who attended this school did not regard each other as equals. Within days of being in the school, it was evident to us that certain groups had more status than did others, especially in the seventh and eighth grades. The higher-status groups were generally the larger ones, and their members were often the topic of conversation by others in the school. In seventh grade, there were two separate popular groups, one made up only of boys, the other of girls. By eighth grade, these two groups had merged to some degree, so that many of the popular boys and girls now sat together at a row of tables at one end of the cafeteria.

Although it was evident from the start that these students were more popular than others, it took us well into the first year of the study to understand what popularity meant at Woodview. Studies of elementary students imply that the popular students are the best-liked. This was definitely not the case in this school.

Instead, we were told that popular people were the most *visible* in the school; they were the students most people knew by name. According to some girls who were not as visible, the nice part about being popular is that "everybody knows you." Students who were more visible explained to us that "the good part [about popularity] is that you get a lot of attention," whereas those who lacked visibility felt that they and their achievements were generally ignored by others. Joyce Canaan also found that visibility was central to popularity for middle school students, meaning that you had lots of people who knew you and wanted to talk with you.[1]

Given Woodview's large size, it would be impossible for all the students to know each other by name. Thus, in many ways it makes sense that being well known would make some people stand out. In sixth grade there were few ways for students to gain visibility. Two of the more attractive girls in the grade were talked about as being popular, but no elite groups existed at this grade level. Instead, there was a greater sense of equality among all students.

When cheerleading and athletic teams were formed in seventh grade there was a basis for some people to gain greater visibility than their peers. Certain athletic games were considered important cultural events and were widely attended by students outside the athletic sphere. This made participants in these events highly visible to the entire student body.

The interest shown by the larger community and the student body in the interscholastic competition of the male athletic teams at Woodview reflects this activity's cultural importance. Crowds for football games ranged from two hundred to five hundred people. Wrestling matches and basketball games did not match these attendance figures but did attract in excess of one hundred persons regularly. Informal groups discussed upcoming games and matches and made plans to attend together, meet at the games, or socialize after the games. Even the athletic players seemed to have more interest in planning postgame activities with friends than in the games themselves. At some level, they realized that they provided important social opportunities for the general student body. Nonparticipants also realized this, which resulted in greater prestige for male athletes throughout the school.

Participants understood that their identities as team members increased their prestige, and they therefore actively attempted to make this identity more visible. Wearing uniforms was a major source of pride for team members. Being allowed to wear their team jerseys was a reward coaches granted players for exceptional effort and performance. Athletes also approved of the official team dress code, which some coaches enforced on game days. In addition, an informal code evolved that included the wearing of particular athletic shoes (or wearing them in a certain manner). Athletes also exhibited pride when wearing a bandage or cast or when using crutches as a result of athletic injuries. Many nonathletes copied the style of dress developed by athletes, but they were often viewed negatively for trying to imitate the athletes' style, since they had not officially earned the right to dress in this manner.

The high status of boys' sports activities was evident in the fact that one had to be an athlete to be a member of the popular group. Self-identification as an athlete was enhanced by associating only with other athletes. Identity as a team member was further enhanced in informal talk by focusing on team activities as topics of conversation.

The high level of interest surrounding boys' athletic events was not present for girls' athletic competition. This was in part because boys' athletic events have a longer history in secondary schools and have gained considerable community support over the years. Woodview helped promote greater interest in boys' athletic events by holding school rallies. Furthermore, some of the male coaches were openly critical of attempts by female coaches to enhance the visibility of female athletics.

> Paulson [a basketball coach] made a comment, "Douglas,
> did you hear that the girl's team was thinking of using it [the
> high school gym]? They want to have their games there."
> Douglas acted really surprised and said, "What for? Why
> would they want to play over there?" Paulson said some-
> thing about better coverage and visibility, and Douglas
> laughed and said, "Do you think they're going to fill it up?"
> This was somewhat sarcastic and, I guess, a reflection on
> the lack of attendance at girls' games. . . . Douglas went on
> to describe what he had seen, saying, "Their offense, their
> offense!" and he would laugh and say, "Their offense is like
> a gym class; two people do something and the other three
> stand around." [Steve's notes]

The lack of faculty and administrative support for female athletics limited their cultural significance in the school. There were
never more than twenty-five students at a girls' athletic event,
and usually there were ten or fewer. As a result of this low
visibility, female athletics did not provide girls with an avenue
for peer status.

Instead, since boys' athletic activities were the most important and most highly attended events in the school, cheerleaders
had considerable visibility among their classmates. Not only did
the cheerleaders get to be seen by large numbers of students at
male basketball and football games, they also performed for the
entire student body at pep rallies and other school activities. In
addition, the fact that there were only seven or eight cheerleaders
per grade served to heighten their visibility further.

As a result, cheerleading was a highly valued activity, especially among the younger girls. Many of the sixth-grade girls
told us they hoped to be cheerleaders next year, and some told
us they wanted to be professional cheerleaders when they grew
up. A large percentage of the girls in the school went to
cheerleading tryout practices; forty-four girls tried out for the

34

sixteen available positions. While practices for cheerleading try-outs were going on, many of the sixth-grade girls spent their lunch period practicing cheers. Girls who were not planning to try out would join in and, on occasion, a boy would try to do some of the stunts.

> A larger number of girls were practicing cheers together. Even Sylvia, who I don't think is going out for cheer-leading, knew all the cheers and could do them. Also, a boy came over and was doing some stunts. It was interest-ing that a boy got involved today as well as the girls in the practicing of stunts. They were very impressed by people who could do a particular thing well like the boy who could touch his toes in the air and Sylvia, who can do the splits both forwards and sideways. [Donna's notes]

In contrast to this boy, who seriously joined in the cheer-leading practice, other boys imitated cheers as a way of mocking this high-status female activity. Even a male coach was observed mocking cheerleaders on one occasion. He told the football play-ers that he'd get them skirts if they wanted to cheer instead of practicing harder. Then he went on to act like a cheerleader with a pompom, saying "Go team go" in a falsetto voice.

Among the girls, there was more agreement about the high status of cheerleaders. In seventh and eighth grades, the popular groups consisted of all or most of the cheerleaders and their friends. Girls were aware that being cheerleaders enhanced their popularity, and they sought to make their cheerleading identity even more visible. For example, on the days of the boys' basket-ball games, many of the cheerleaders who were on the gymnastic team would skip practice and get dressed in their cheerleading uniforms in order to present themselves in the role of cheerleader for as long a period as possible. The cheerleaders also wore their cheerleading shirts to school on certain special occasions, and some even had T-shirts made with the word *cheerleader* printed on the back. In contrast, when the volleyball team members were allowed to wear their volleyball shirts to school on the day of a game, one of the members, who was also a member of the popular group, did not wear her shirt. It appeared that she did not want to endanger her position in the popular group by making her association with the volleyball team too visible.

Differing Views on Social Rankings

As these students experienced this new, more complex level of social ranking, they expressed a range of views about its legitimacy. Although boys disagreed with each other to some degree, most were accepting of the use of athletic ability to determine one's athletic opportunities, such as making a particular team or being part of the starting lineup. For example, one day a group of football players was discussing whether it was fair that the second- and third-string football players usually did not get to play. Initially, some boys felt that their lack of playing caused the nonstarters to perform more poorly than the starting lineup. This viewpoint was challenged by others, who felt that these boys lacked the ability and effort to play better, justifying the legitimacy of the sports' hierarchy.

> This became a discussion of how bad the second and third stringers were. There was somewhat of an ideological debate of how good they should be. George's and Ron's opinion seemed to be that they never get to play and that's why they are no good. Tony, Bryan, and to a certain degree, Chris, said the reason that they don't get to play is that they *are* no good. Bryan was sort of the

spokesman for this group and even stood up while he made his point, saying, "Well, those guys shouldn't be messin' around in practice. They oughta be at practice learnin' so they can play instead of standin' around pickin' their butt. They just stand around and do nothin' and when they get the chance they go in there and act like dummies." Everybody agreed with this and they mentioned somebody named Jack Nelson in particular. They got down on this guy quite a bit. [Steve's notes]

Whether or not these boys were correct in their belief that sports activities represent a true meritocracy, it had important implications for their general acceptance of social hierarchies. Since all the boys in the popular group were members of athletic teams and thus perceived to have strong athletic skills, few boys questioned the legitimacy of the male social rankings.[2] Demonstration of other strengths, such as physical and verbal fighting skills, use of humor, and willingness to be daring and defy politeness norms, further enhanced the likelihood of being in the top group. Again, the sense that certain boys had strengths that others lacked tended to limit the degree of resentment expressed toward popular boys.

Girls were much more likely to express dissatisfaction with social rankings, and especially with the popular girls. Only a small proportion of the student body had the opportunity to participate in the elite activity of cheerleading. Cheerleading selection itself was not considered as clear-cut as athletic competition. Some girls expressed confusion about why certain cheerleaders were selected. Others were very critical of those girls who were selected, commenting negatively on their appearance as well as their performance.

The fact that the rest of the top group consisted primarily of friends of cheerleaders made the social hierarchy seem even more arbitrary. When some eighth-grade girls in a medium-high-status group were asked about factors that influenced popularity, they expressed their confusion to us by saying "We're nice and we wear nice clothes, so how come we're not more popular?" Since these girls relied so much on the friendliness of popular girls to gain higher status, they were often extremely upset when they were ignored by one of these girls. In addition, cheerleaders were often viewed as being snobs because some cheerleaders abandoned former friends to join the popular group. Given the importance of social ties for gaining status, this type of behavior created much more resentment among the girls than it did among the boys.[3]

While most viewed popular girls as being stuck-up, occasionally the snobbishness of these girls was the subject of open debate. For example, one day the name of a cheerleader came up in a conversation of sixth-graders, and immediately someone called her a snob. When Natalie disagreed with this assessment, Andrea went on to give a more extended explanation of why some people might consider this particular girl to be stuck-up.

Sixth Grade[4]

ANDREA: I don't—I just can't believe it. I mean usually she's sittin' with Jane May and those guys you know. [Brief discussion to identify who she is referring to.]
STEPHANIE: Where's Jane May? [They point to her.]
LAURA: [Unclear] she's a snob.
NATALIE: I don't think she's a snob.
ANDREA: Huh?
NATALIE: I don't think she's a snob.
ANDREA: I don't think she's a snob either. It's just I don't like her. [Laughs.]
LAURA: [Unclear] I don't care if other people like her I just—it's my opinion.
ANDREA: The thing that uhm the thing that people are jealous of her—girl—other girls are jealous of her. They say you know like uh they don't like her because uh uhm

because she's pretty and all the boys like her and they think that she's stuck-up. She's really not. She's really very nice.

Andrea believed that this girl was being labeled a snob because others were jealous of her, not because of her actual behavior. This shows that some popular girls might be unfairly judged as a result of general resentment about the status hierarchy.

High-status girls talked to us about the disadvantages of being in a popular group. One girl reported that because popular girls are viewed as being stuck-up, other kids are "kind of scared of them and they don't know their real personality." Other cheerleaders told us they felt it was unfair that they were labeled stuck-up, whereas popular boys were liked by everyone. Although these girls did not consider themselves stuck-up, they later expressed an unwillingness to associate with lower-status people.

One thing that came up right away was that they said that since they became cheerleaders (or popular—the two words are practically synonymous to them) that a lot of girls were jealous and that they were called "stuck-up" or "Little Miss Priss" a lot. Carrie said that people had gone so far as to make up and spread rumors about her that weren't true. Darlene brought up the point that it wasn't fair because it was the popular girls who were treated like this and the popular boys were not, that people simply liked them. . . . The bell rang and I asked if I could sit with them at lunch sometime and they said yes. I asked where they usually sat, if it was usually on the gym side of the cafeteria. They said, "Oh we *never* sit on the other side." I asked why not and they said, "That's where all the *grits* sit." [Cathy's notes]

In general, the greater association between popularity and friendship among girls made popularity appear more arbitrary and less merited. This contributed to much greater resentment among the girls, leading to the beginning of a reverse status hierarchy in which high-status girls are disliked almost as much as low-status girls.[5]

The Complex Dynamics of Social Class

The social ranking that developed within this school was influenced largely by the extracurricular activities, but in complex ways it was also related to the students' social class background.[6] Many of the students came from middle-class and upper-working-class backgrounds. Others came from lower-working-class, often rural, backgrounds and were negatively referred to as the "grits" (a reference to being tough and "gritty"). Although a few lower-working-class boys were on the football team and occasionally sat with the popular group, most lower-working-class students sat on the opposite side of the cafeteria, especially in the seventh and eighth grade.

In many ways *grit* was a label by default. Students viewed as deviant by certain popular students were considered grits. For example, if a boy was not involved in sports he lacked an important basis for participating in conversations in the high-status groups. Other students were viewed as deviant because they displayed a lack of concern with school officials and values or because of their physical appearance and dress. The "grit" label generally implied the person was a loser in the struggle for social status. Certain boys might be feared because of their propensity toward violence, but they were not respected. This social ranking was reinforced by school officials as well as within the daily interactions of students. Many people who sat on the same side of the cafeteria as the most popular students viewed everyone on the other side of the cafeteria as being grits. People on the low-status side did not necessarily give themselves this label, however, and instead referred only to certain people as grits. For example, one girl told us that a grit was "somebody who smokes marijuana and sleeps with just about any boy."

At the same time, some people who sat on the low-status side viewed all of the people on the other side as being stuck-up. The same process that took place among girls regarding the members of the popular group also seemed to take place among girls regarding the two different sides of the cafeteria. No one explained precisely why some people sat on one side rather than the other, but it seemed to be due in part to a sense that people from certain social class backgrounds wanted to avoid contact with lower-class people. In return, lower-class people wanted to avoid people they believed to be stuck-up.

Eighth-Grade Interview with Donna
JULIE: And those kids who are poor and can't afford expensive clothes sit over there. [Points to the other side of the cafeteria]
BONNIE: Most of them. That's why Nancy's over there cleaning off the tables.
JULIE: [Laughs]
DONNA: How does that get started? How does it get started that certain people sit over there and certain people sit at this table?
BONNIE: Like if there's a gross dirty kid that came and sat by this girl that was real clean and everything she'd go, "Oh, gross. You smell," or something like that. So they'd get up and go over there and most of those guys over there think that everybody over here is a snob and they don't want to sit by them.
JULIE[?]:   Most of them are.

This desire to avoid classmates on the high-status side of the cafeteria presented problems when low-status students were assigned to that side of the cafeteria for clean-up duty.[7]

> As the lunch went on she [Kerry, a low-status student] said that she would really hate to work over there [on the high-status side] and that if she couldn't get out of it she was going to pretend to be sick and throw up so she could get out of it, because she was just not going to work over there. She said she didn't like anybody over there and that nobody liked her who sat over there. After I questioned her as to why, she said, "I don't know. They're just stuck-up." [Cathy's notes]

The fear of being ridiculed or mistreated by high-status students was incredibly strong for this particular girl, who was willing to do anything to avoid having to associate with them. This suggests that the general social ranking within the school was extremely rigid. As one girl put it, "It's like segregation of unpopular people and popular people."

Despite the strong influence of social class on social rankings within the school, students' views on the legitimacy of class stratification differed and were quite complex. It is clear from some of the preceding discussion that some people assumed that social class was a legitimate basis for discriminating against others—that it was normal not to want to sit near grits or someone who didn't wear the same type of clothes or was perceived to have a different standard of cleanliness.[8] Ellen Brantlinger also found that few friendships crossed social class boundaries in her study of middle and high school students.[9] At the same time, it is also clear that many of the lower-status students resented their higher-status classmates and referred to them as being snobbish. This resentment indicates that people who were at the other end of this hierarchy did not see social class as a legitimate or fair basis for social ranking because it was something over which they have little control.

Furthermore, class-based elitism was compounded by its association with urban snobbishness. Since many lower-income youths came from rural areas, they were ridiculed for habits related to a different lifestyle as well as for their lack of name-brand or new clothes. These elitist attitudes, however, were not shared by all students. In the following example, Andrea complains about her classmate's snobbish attitude toward the rural lifestyles.

> And then Nicki talked quite a bit about the fact that this guy Tommy milks cows and then drinks the milk without sterilizing it or anything. At this point, Andrea said that was okay; that she had spent a year living on her grandmother's farm and they had done that. Nicki said, "But yeah, but you sterilized the milk." And she said, "No, we never boiled it or anything." Nicki was kind of grossed out by that. Later Andrea came over to me and said, "Can you believe what Nicki said about drinking milk?" Andrea thought that it was a real snotty thing for Nicki to do to talk about how gross it is to drink fresh milk. She went on and on about it, "I just can't believe she said that! It shows what a stuck-up attitude she has." Then she added something like, "That's what you get coming from a rich family." Then Elaine walked up later and Andrea said to her, "Can you believe what Nicki said?" Elaine said, "About what?" She said, "About milk. Drinking milk." Elaine was a bit more noncommittal about it. [Stephanie's notes]

All of these girls sat on the low-status side of the cafeteria. It is interesting that even among these girls there were clear differences in attitudes about what is offensive behavior as well as what is snobbish behavior. While Nicki considered it all right to put someone down for drinking nonpasteurized fresh milk, Andrea viewed this as simply a different lifestyle and saw Nicki's attitude as reflecting her snobbishness.

Equally complex was the negative view toward elitism among the high-status youth. Although many of these students did not recognize the inherent elitism in their own behaviors, they were often openly critical of students they perceived as being upper class. In one group, the student from the wealthiest background had trouble making any friends because others were always commenting on her family background. In the group of popular boys, the heaviest teasing that went on during the course of the entire year was based on one member's perceived snobbishness when he moved from the locker he was sharing with a group member to another locker.

I was greeted by Joe as I sat down. As soon as I sat down they started talking about how Mike was too upper class to sit with them. Joe was the most active in this. He asked Mike if he was sure he didn't mind "all us grits" sitting with him. When he said this he was laughing a lot, as was Eric. Mike sat in silence and looked like he didn't want to have to deal with this. This went on a while and I finally asked how come they were blowing Mike so much grief. Mike said that it started when he moved out of the locker he was sharing with Joe. Joe said it was because he thought he was too good for him while Mike said it had something to do with the location of the locker. . . . Eric started talking about all the "Polo" stuff that Mike had. I don't ever remember Mike wearing much designer stuff but I just listened.[10] Eric said that Mike wore "Polo" socks and underwear and "Polo" garters to hold up his socks. . . . Eric started talking about the mansion Mike lived in and Mike denied it was a mansion, saying it wasn't even as big as the two-story house that Eric had.

Since Mike was not responding playfully, the teasing escalated into ridicule and continued for much of the lunch period, until finally Mike became so upset he resorted to physical aggression.

> Joe kept talking about how upper class Mike was and finally Mike reached over the table and swung at him two or three times. He hit him in the chest but not hard enough to cause any damage. When this happened I noticed that everyone within twenty-five feet of our table was watching to see what would happen next. Mike sat back down and told Joe he was going to kick his ass. He was real upset, and Hank asked if he was going to cry. Mike said no, and I don't think he was, but he was real upset. He broke a pencil into three of four pieces. [Steve's notes]

This incident reflects a negative orientation toward people who act is if they are better than others, in this case by wearing designer clothes or refusing to associate with people with less money. Mike's background was not that different from other group members and, as he tried to explain, his background had nothing to do with his desire to change lockers. Yet, he was extremely sensitive to the accusation of elitism and, while he could handle some other types of teasing by these boys, he lost control of his anger when accused of snobbishness.

This example indicates a complex attitude toward social class among some of the youth at this school. Although an elitist attitude toward lower-working-class and rural students was so ingrained that it was not even recognized by many students, these same students often accused their classmates of having elitist attitudes. This phenomenon could reflect the fact that Woodview had a very large working-class student body and that students were aware that other schools in town had a larger middle-class student body. Overall, it suggests that social class has a complex effect on students' attitudes regarding hierarchies, so that students tend to view their own position as being a legitimate one, but view those above them as having unfair advantages.

The Dynamics of Race

Social class was much more closely related to status processes in this school than was race, in part because only a small number of Afro-American students attended the school. They came from different social class backgrounds and were as likely as Euro-American students to participate in cheerleading and athletics. Thus, Afro-American students were found at every level of the status hierarchy, except for the very lowest level, which happened to be entirely Euro-American.

Even though racial discrimination in the community and larger society was not directly reflected in the social rankings at Woodview, it was evident at times in the peer activities of students. Boys on the low-status side of the cafeteria often told racist jokes and occasionally targeted particular black students in their parodies.[11] In the incident described here a group of boys began to mock a classmate's hairstyle after someone realized his hair was standing up in a fashion similar to that of a black girl in the school.

> Andrea came up and said hello to everyone and rubbed Jeff's hair so it all stood up. Walter laughed, and Jeff, realizing how it looked, stood up and said, "My name is Karla West. Look at me. My name is Karla West." He said it loud enough for a lot of people to hear, and I noticed that people from a couple of different tables were laughing. Then Walter pointed to the end of our table and

said that Karla was sitting down there. I looked and fig-
ured out who she was. All the girls she was with were
laughing, and so was she. For the rest of the lunch period
Jeff would stand up and do this every so often, and by
the end of the period it had regressed toward racial over-
tones. He started using more of a black dialect when he
did it, and Ken, Jack, and Walter started to tell racist
jokes. . . . A black guy walked by, and Walter started calling him Sambo. The guy turned and looked but kept
walking. Walter said that if Karla were taller she could
mop the ceiling. Finally, some food started being thrown
from our area to the area Karla was in. I was embarrassed
but stayed. Tracy [a black cheerleader] was with Karla's
group and told Jeff to quit making such a fool of himself.
Jeff laughed at this and acted more like a fool by talking
funny and addressing nonsensical comments toward
Tracy. [Steve's notes]

The parody of Karla began with a simple imitation of her
hairstyle. It is interesting, and revealing of how racial attitudes
become normalized, that everyone found this initial parody humorous. It is not clear how Karla really felt, but she, too, went
along with it at first. Not until the incident became more explicitly racist was it challenged by another black student. Her position as a cheerleader gave her considerable status over this group
of lower-status males. Her challenge was not enough to completely stop their behavior, but it did diffuse it. Having the skills
to diffuse racist messages, however, does not mean that students
are not harmed by them.

Incidents such as this were relatively rare at Woodview, but
a black student who attended another middle school in the same
community told us that she and her sister faced racial insults on
almost a daily basis. These insults ranged from explicit comments about their skin color to negative labels such as "porch

monkey" and "nigger." The relatively greater frequency of such insults in this school may be due to the more isolated status of these two students, who described themselves as being very shy, and/or the absence of adult researchers. Taken together, these incidents show how the racism of the larger community and society can intervene in students' lives at any point.

In addition, black students at Woodview often had to struggle to gain and maintain acceptance in their smaller friendship groups. Some were clearly regarded as outsiders and constantly had to develop new strategies in order to be included in the daily conversations and rituals of the peer groups. Occasionally, within groups or on athletic teams, there were tensions in which it was clear that racial differences played a part. For example, several people on the volleyball team became upset with a black teammate during the middle of the season, claiming that she bossed them around too much and called them names like "lemon lips," a derogatory term for whites. This conflict was discussed openly during a practice session, with the coach present. At the end of the discussion, the black girl offered to leave the team if they wanted her to, but her teammates assured her that this was not what they wanted. One of the girls later said that she only brought up the incident because her father told her that she should, warning her that it could result in her getting "the crap beat out of you." This suggests that racial tension in the larger community influenced the way racial conflicts were dealt with in the school.

In general, their vulnerable position as outsiders meant that Afro-American students had to work to maintain group acceptance. None of these students was among the smallest percentage of students who had no friends or group affiliation, but they were clearly aware of the negative experience of those students. In fact, when two researchers (Cathy and I) started coming to the lunchroom, Afro-American students were among the first to invite us to join their groups. Being on the outside themselves, they seemed particularly aware of the importance of finding some way to fit in with a group and avoid the ridicule encountered by isolates.

Targeting the Low End of
the Hierarchy

The students who most dramatically felt the negative impact of the school status hierarchy were those at the very bottom. At each grade level, three to five students became identified as having characteristics with which most students wanted to avoid being associated.[12] Often these characteristics reflected gender concerns such as perceived unattractiveness in girls and atypical gender behavior in both boys and girls. Other undesirable factors were perceived low intelligence and unusual behavior; this made special education students more likely candidates for social isolation.

Students often deal with their insecurities by scapegoating others whom they view as being even more deficient than themselves. By creating a group of isolates at the bottom of the status continuum, most students at least have the assurance that they are not as unpopular or as abnormal as some of their classmates. Like the popular students, isolates also become highly visible in the school setting. For them, however, visibility is painful and often embarrassing—a source of unwanted negative attention rather than the positive attention and esteem received by their popular peers.

Many isolates were also subject to some form of sexual ridicule.[13] The most common form of sexual insulting or ridicule in this school was the use of homosexual labels such as *faggot* and *queer*. (See chapters 6 and 8 for more discussion about this.) Since many youth have some anxiety about homosexuality, one way to deal with this anxiety is to attach the homosexual label to students they consider to be least like themselves, that is, isolates.

Ted pointed to a girl in line and said she was in Special Ed and that she was always getting picked on. As I saw

49

> her in line I noticed three or four people circled around
> her. They were laughing and exchanging comments, but
> the girl in the middle did not appear to be enjoying her-
> self. Ted said her problem was that she liked girls. "You
> know, one of those kinds." When I asked what kind he
> said, "You know, kind of queer." [Steve's notes]

In some cases, isolates were even forced to conform to the homosexual label. One day Molly said that she had seen Nellie, an
isolate and a special education student, kiss another special education student in the stairwell. Her friend Janice responded by
saying, "Well, that's because they told her they would kick her
ass in if she didn't!" By ridiculing isolates in this manner, students ensured that homosexuality became more solidly associated with social rejection. This in turn very likely increased the
degree of homophobia among the students.

Students also ridiculed female isolates by making fun of
their perceived unattractiveness, in particular, their lack of sexual
attractiveness to boys. A common way to do this was for boys to
convey their romantic interest in a particular isolate and then
make fun if she took it seriously. This type of ridicule extended
to accusations that isolates had slept with particular boys, or even
gotten pregnant by them.

> Several students said to Theresa, "Theresa, did you have
> a baby with Donnie?" Theresa just smiled and shook her
> head, and I looked over and sort of smiled at her. Then
> Sharon explained to me that this is the same Donnie that
> she had gone with and he had asked Theresa to go with
> him as a joke, but she had taken it seriously. She said that
> now they really make fun of her and that she's easy to
> make fun of because she'll start to cry. Sharon said if she
> doesn't watch out, Theresa's going to be loony when she
> gets out of here. [Stephanie's notes]

Theresa was initially ridiculed because she was considered unattractive, not because of an emotional handicap. Here a student expresses concern that Theresa might *become* loony as a result of the ridicule she faced at school. There is increasing awareness in the popular press that ridicule of isolates is extremely damaging to their psychological well-being, sometimes leading to suicide. By scapegoating these isolates, the anxiety of the general student population is focused on a few students who end up experiencing very high levels of social distress. Two college students who were isolates in middle school reported being so numb and overwhelmed at the time that they didn't know what to do. One student shared this poem, which she wrote when she was fourteen:

> i stand alone
> and out of reach
> fragile, like
> a piece of glass
> if they touch me
> i will break
> and so i let
> their torment pass
> i hide behind
> the windowpane
> and pray that
> they will let me be
> for now i fear
> that i've become
> a prisoner
> inside of me

This poem reveals the way some isolates cope with daily ridicule—by retreating farther inside themselves.

One might think that students who experience ridicule would be less inclined to make fun of others, but this does not seem to be the case.[14] Although Billy was ridiculed and pushed around by his peers, he himself made fun of certain isolates, such as Jenny. In the following instance, Billy at first defended Jenny's intelligence, but then, in an attempt to be included in group camaraderie, he joined in the gossip by derisively imitating her.

> Pat told me a story about how someone in her group had hit a girl and then she pointed out the girl, who was Jenny. She said that she was "retarded." Billy said, "She can't be too retarded, she reads books." Pat replied, "She's pretty retarded." Then Billy started giving his imitation of a retarded person, acting like he was asking questions about how to get around in the school, acted really stupid, sort of stuttered his words. [Cathy's notes]

By joining the group's ridicule of Jenny, Billy was able both to redirect his own insecurities outward and to deflect potential negative attention from himself.

Some people did attempt to stop the open ridicule of isolates. Most of the successful attempts were made by girls who were starting to define such ridicule as rude and insensitive. As early as sixth grade, girls began to reprimand their peers, claiming that they were taking the right of free speech too far. In one incident, an overweight isolate had asked a sixth-grader if she could borrow some money.

> When I came back, Andrea was reprimanding Ilene. They explained that . . . while I was away . . . Gloria had walked up to Andrea and had asked Andrea to loan her some money. Before Andrea could say anything, Ilene had said, "Well, she'll lend you some money, but not money that you're gonna eat more with!" This made Andrea angry that Ilene was so rude to Gloria, and caused a full-fledged fight between them. . . . Andrea got more

and more angry, to the point where she started yelling at Ilene, saying, "If you open your trap once more and say that kind of thing. . . . That was really rude. Everybody else has the right to live! Sure there's freedom of speech but you're taking it too far!" [Stephanie's notes]

As girls began to feel that the emotional costs to isolates of being openly ridiculed were too great, they encouraged their friends only to make fun of isolates behind their backs. Gossip of this nature would still allow them to detach themselves from isolates.

At one point they saw Wendy, who is a very tall girl who may have some social problems as people tend to make fun of her. Mardi was sort of making fun of her openly and said, "Let's all tell Wendy how nice she looks." Then she got Wendy's attention and told her that she looked nice. Laura said in a kidding way that it was mean to do that, showing that she wasn't really mad at Mardi but did think it was mean. Laura said that it was okay to make fun of her behind her back but they shouldn't do it in front of her because she probably took the remark seriously. [Donna's notes]

Comments such as these seemed to be effective in reducing the amount of open ridicule among girls. By eighth grade, incidents of such ridicule still occurred among girls but were relatively rare. Boys seldom questioned the appropriateness of ridiculing isolates—once, two boys discussed how special education students should be left alone because "it wasn't their fault," and on another occasion, two boys debated whether it was appropriate to pretend to flatter a female isolate. Thus, there was little reduction in the amount of ridicule by boys over the three years of middle school.

Some unpopular students minimized the amount of ridicule they received by becoming verbally aggressive, challenging other students before those others had a chance to ridicule them. Two special education students relied on this strategy. Martha tried to figure out what name would make a particular student "madder than hell" and then would repeatedly call that classmate by this name, while Trudy relied on standard name-calling.

> I noticed today how Trudy would loudly shout at various non–special education females as they walked past, "What are you looking at, you bitch?!" and other antisocial remarks to that effect. Perhaps they *were* looking at her, because it seemed to basically be the same few people that she would shout at. I've seen her do this before. [Cathy's notes]

Trudy's and Martha's behavior was successful in reducing ridicule from others. Since aggressive behavior in girls was viewed negatively by most students, however, this strategy was possibly only effective in eliminating the more extreme consequences of peer rejection. Several studies have found that rejected youth are viewed as hostile and likely to initiate fights.[15] This perception may increase the level of rejection toward these students, but it appears from the examples we observed that young people may engage in hostile behavior as a *response* to being rejected.

In general, isolates had few ways to escape from their position of being the most unpopular students in the school, since so few people were willing to associate with them.[16] Although certain verbal strategies minimized the degree of ridicule they faced, the main problem stemmed from other students' desire to find someone with lower status than themselves whom they could ridicule or mock. This suggests a high degree of insecurity among many youth in the school over their own social standing.

The Complex Nature
of Social Rankings

It is evident that students at Woodview were strongly influenced by social ranking within the school and within the larger society. Had this school not provided opportunities for certain students to have more visibility than others through participation in elite activities, such as cheerleading, football, and basketball, clear popular groups might not have emerged. The lack of any distinct popular groups in the sixth grade, where these activities were not offered, supports this idea. At the same time, the overall stratification of high- and low-status students reflected a social class division as well as the division of popular versus nonpopular groups. This division was also not as strong in sixth grade, suggesting that school hierarchies both furthered and reflected social rankings in the larger society.

There are some possible explanations for the close relationship between these two bases of social ranking. For one thing, certain activities such as cheerleading required a substantial family income. Although the school provided some financial support for cheerleading activities, cheerleaders' parents were expected to purchase two outfits and pay for their daughters to attend an annual summer cheerleading camp. Athletic activities required that parents be able to transport their children after school and not depend on their labor during athletic season. This could limit the number of low-income boys and/or boys from rural backgrounds who were able to participate on male athletic teams. In addition, students from low-income families probably did not have important earlier opportunities to participate in gymnastics, basketball, or other activities that would have improved their chance to succeed in cheerleading or sports tryouts.

Race was not as directly related to the overall status hierarchy, but being part of a small minority increased the likelihood that Afro-Americans would feel like outsiders within their peer groups. Afro-American youth at Woodview successfully avoided being isolates by using a number of strategies to reduce racial tension and gain inclusion into groups. Being able to diffuse racist comments successfully does not mean they are without harm to the students who must deal with them.

It is also important to study isolates within the context of other status processes. Psychologists have tried to account for peer rejection by focusing on those who were rejected, and in particular on their lack of positive social skills.[17] Recently, other researchers have given more attention to environmental factors that contribute to peer rejection, arguing that peer rejection may more accurately reflect the interactional dynamics of high-status children than the social skills of low-status children.[18] Other studies have also pointed to the importance of the overall school environment for one particular type of isolate—special education students. For example, mentally handicapped students who were mainstreamed rather than being placed in self-contained class-rooms were somewhat more likely to be rejected by peers.[19] When mainstreamed learning-disabled students made up more than one-fourth of the class, however, they were more likely to be accepted by their nondisabled peers than were other main-streamed students.[20] This indicates that the school context in which special education students are placed can have a powerful influence on the degree of acceptance they receive.

Still other studies point to the importance of overall social relations within the classroom or school setting. In one other study of elementary classrooms, Maureen Hallinan found that there were more extremely popular and extremely unpopular students in traditional classrooms than in open classrooms.[21] Other studies have found that students relate more positively toward mentally handicapped students in classrooms that emphasize a cooperative rather than a competitive style of learning.[22] Finally, smaller schools and schools that do not offer only a few highly visible extracurricular activities, such as alternative schools, are less likely to have isolates.[23] Such schools sometimes also offer forums for discussing social concerns such as repeated teasing and/or ridicule of a student, thereby breaking into the vicious cycles found in this school.

The fact that Woodview inadvertently created a scarce resource by giving so few students a chance to become visible created a very competitive atmosphere, which may have contributed to the high degree of rejection and ridicule of isolates. Many of the students who attended this school were later interviewed as part of a study of high school peer cultures. They reported that the middle school cliques were so rigid and so restricted that only a few students could be in popular groups, while the rest perceived themselves to be "dweebs" and "nerds." In high school, they found that they had many more opportunities to get involved in extracurricular activities and to gain a sense of meaningful group acceptance, making them feel much more socially competent.[24] Some high school students also reported being less intimidated by classmates in other groups, and high school students in general had more contact across cliques.[25]

Most students in this school tried to avoid being isolates and sought greater recognition from their peers, but they expressed some ambivalence about the status processes going on around them. This was especially true for girls, who perceived the status system to be quite arbitrary. By referring to popular girls as snobs, they were in essence saying that these girls were unwilling to spend time with them because of the "snobby" girls' elitist attitudes rather than their own deficiencies. This reverse status ranking, attributing negative traits to those at the top of the ranking, is an initial stage in the process of resisting social rankings and their implied evaluations.

As students get older, reverse status ranking becomes stronger. By high school, students who were not members of the "preppy" or "trendy" cliques were even more vocal about their negative evaluations of these cliques, saying that students in them were too materialistic, or that they followed every trend without ever thinking for themselves.[26] A British study also found that working-class boys grow increasingly disdainful of their middle-class peers, whom they perceive as being passive, boring, and less sexually competent.[27]

Students at Woodview have an interesting and complex view of social class, combining disdain for elitism with complacency about their own class standing. Their complacency may reflect in part the subtle nature of many social class status processes in this country, which often give the impression that all job and career opportunities are based upon merit. However, the fact that many of these students expressed some disdain for elitism suggests that at least some are aware that social class processes are often arbitrary.

It would be interesting to know what factors contribute to greater resistance toward social class and other social hierarchies as people get older. In this school, the boys' social hierarchy received little criticism, in part because male popularity was perceived to be based on merit. It may be that as individuals encounter more cases where ranking decisions appear arbitrary or even unfair, they begin to develop greater skepticism about the legitimacy of such decisions and the entire ranking system.

In summary, these students were just beginning to examine their position within a more complex social ranking. Consequently, they were quite concerned with gaining peer recognition and avoiding peer rejection. It is within this context that both boys and girls were constructing notions of what it means to be a male or female, both among themselves and in regard to the opposite sex. Within this construction we will see that yet another hierarchy emerged—that of gender inequality. The fact that most students in this school were somewhat insecure about their social standing may help to explain why so few students were willing to risk appearing "abnormal" by challenging more traditional gender messages. Instead, most students' first priority was to be included by their peers and to participate in the informal speech routines of their groups, regardless of the impact of their participation. Not only did this encourage boys to engage in sexist behaviors at times, but in some cases girls also engaged in behaviors that promoted limiting and negative perceptions of themselves as girls.

5

Tough Guys,
Wimps, and Weenies

The boys in this study live in a society that places considerable importance on men being aggressive and tough. The mass media, especially movies and television, offer them many models of aggressiveness being esteemed and valued. Within the school context, male athletics was an arena in which coaches promoted the value and importance of toughness.[1] During wrestling practices boys were told to make their opponents hurt—"make him suffer"—and not to be a "puss" or "noodle." There was also an explicit emphasis on developing a mean attitude, implying that niceness was an effeminate trait.

During the drills Coach Adams emphasized being meaner than they had been before. He said that he wanted animals but that he had a bunch of "nice boys." When he said "nice boys" he paused and softened his voice. [Steve's notes]

Football coaches also emphasized the importance of hitting hard in order to win games. If the team lost, coaches often said it was due to their team's lack of physical aggression. On the other hand, when players were physically confrontational in the context of a game, they were praised.

> I said that I had heard that Coach Paulson wasn't pleased with the way the team played. Walter and Carl both agreed. Walter [the team manager] said that the team didn't hit like they should have and that made the coach mad. Carl said, "Yeah, but I really socked that guy. Man, I threw him down on the concrete. Did you hear Coach James yelling, "Way to go, Orville [his nickname]?" [Steve's notes]

Coaches at this school did not condone physical fighting outside of the context of sports, but at times they approved the use of physical force to deal with interpersonal conflict, as long as it occurred on the playing field.

> A player came up to a coach as practice was just beginning and complained that another player was starting a fight with him. The coach seemed aggravated at having to deal with this and told him to "knock his socks off in practice." The player was not satisfied with the suggestion but realized that was all he could get from him. [Steve's notes]

Similarly, adult athletes studied by Michael Messner describe how they learned to view aggression as a normal part of

62

sports such as football, as reflected in this statement by a professional football player. "When I first started playing, if I would hit a guy hard and he wouldn't get up, it would bother me. [But] when I was a sophomore in high school, first game, I knocked out two quarterbacks, and people loved it. The coach loved it. Everybody loved it. The more you play, the more you realize that it is just a part of the game—somebody's gonna get hurt. It could be you, it could be him—most of the time it's better if it's him."[2]

The boys themselves often conveyed the importance of toughness through ritual insults. Many of the names the boys used to insult each other imply some form of weakness such as "pud," "squirt," and "wimp." Other names, such as "pussy," "girl," "fag," and "queer," associate lack of toughness directly with femininity or homosexuality. These names are used when boys fail to meet certain standards of combativeness.

This type of insulting was particularly common among the athletes in the high-status group, who used it to reinforce the importance of being aggressive on the playing field or wrestling mat. For example, one day a group of boys were insulting two of their friends. First, Eric told Tom that he'd have to be a "real wuss" to let Kevin beat him in wrestling. Then Kevin insulted Eric, saying that he didn't even come out for wrestling because he was a "pussy" and that he should have hit more people during football instead of just standing and pushing at them.

On another day, this same group of boys used homosexual labels to reinforce the importance of stoic invulnerability when gossiping about boys who weren't present.

Hank yelled for some guy to stay away from Jennifer. He said to the group, "That guy's a fag. What a jerk," and everyone agreed that he was a fag. Then Eric said that Mike was turning into a fag. His reasoning was that he didn't want to get hit in practice anymore. Every time he got hit he would get mad at the guy that did it. [Steve's notes]

Raphela Best has noted how boys within peer groups become increasingly important sources of influence for "policing masculinity."[3] In her study of middle school students, Joyce Canaan also found that top-group boys established a sense of masculine superiority by telling jokes and insulting low-group boys, especially those who were overweight.[4] Homosexual insults were often directed toward boys who fail to engage in stereotypical masculine behavior.[5] Since these labels are viewed so negatively by adolescent boys, their extensive use suggests that strong pressure is needed to reinforce traditional masculine behavior. This pressure would not be necessary if the traditional male role was as desirable as many have claimed it is. In other words, if boys naturally desired to be tough, competitive, and aggressive, they would not need such strong peer pressure to do so.

Many of the collaborative stories told by boys also conveyed messages about the importance of physical force. Stories about their common experiences in football games and wrestling meets often included bragging about incidents in which they had displayed their aggressiveness by hurting or intimidating an opponent. This tough orientation was also carried to other sports such as soccer, where antagonistic behavior often involved breaking the official game rules. For example, one day Mark described how he purposely waited for the ball to go by in soccer games; then, as the opponent was running, he would kick him in the shins. Then Hank described how he had grabbed the ball and thrown it into the kicker's face, getting away with this rule violation.

Besides telling stories in which they highlighted their own combative behavior, boys occasionally told stories about peers who demonstrated a high degree of forceful domination. In the following example, a star wrestler is the topic of a collaborative story.

Paul also talked about Sonny's match in the [wrestling] meet last night and how Sonny was clearly the superior wrestler. He said that he embarrassed and humiliated the guy on the mat. It seems that he was slapping his hand and stomping around out there. In telling the story, Paul himself acted it out by getting up, taking a wrestling stance, and making certain attempts at two-legged and one-legged take-downs and flying sprawls which Sonny had done the night before. Paul thought this was very funny, and others enjoyed it and added to it as well. [Steve's notes]

The content of this story conveys the importance of being physically forceful and shows that humiliating an opponent is seen as an especially desirable behavior.

Joint storytelling allowed boys to further refine the meaning of toughness by bringing up different aspects of it within the same story. In general, collaborative narration is a highly flexible mode of talk that allows students to represent many different aspects of a common concern by acting out the roles of other participants as well as their own roles.[6] For example, one day Sam began a story in which he presented himself as being stoic enough to sustain a serious injury during a football game. His friends, however, used the same performance to cast him in a more negative, less tough role.

Seventh Grade

SAM: Hey Joe, remember when I told ya, I go, "My finger hurt so bad I can't even feel it"? He goes, "Good, you won't feel 'em hit it." [Laughter] He didn't know I'd broke it, man. You remember in the Edgewood game, I broke my finger?

HANK: I called him a big pussy when he told me that. "Hey, you big pussy, get out there 'n' play."

SAM: He [referring to the coach] goes, "Don't worry, you won't feel it when they hit it."
HANK: Sam goes, Sam goes, "Look at my finger." [In a high voice] I said, "Oh, you pussy cat, you can't play."
SAM: *You liar.*
HANK: I did too |
SAM: |Well I did, I played the whole game.
TOM: [To Sam] You was cryin' too.
SAM: Yes I did man.

After Sam offered a positive, tough identity for himself, Hank claimed an even stronger identity for himself, saying, "Hey, you big pussy, get out there 'n' play." This "coachlike" talk is used to intimidate and thereby toughen players who are not willing to give their full effort under any circumstance. Hank thus implied that Sam was in need of more "manliness" than he was demonstrating. However, Sam did not or chose not to pick up on this negative implication and instead joined in by also casting Hank into the role of a "tough, unyielding coach." Hank then further developed a weak, feminine identity for Sam by casting him in the role of a whiner, using a high intonation to convey his negative view of this role.

Thus, through this brief but complicated co-narration, these boys reveal how they interpret several different aspects of toughness. Through taking on different identities and casting others in various roles, these boys are able to demonstrate their orientation toward many different dimensions of this valued characteristic. For example, Sam is portrayed by himself and others as measuring up in that he did sustain a serious injury during an athletic event and continued to play despite the injury. At the same time, he is found lacking by at least one boy who believed that he needed some form of intimidation to make him carry out this tough behavior. Sam also was not able to mask his pain sufficiently; he apparently drew undue attention to his injury and cried. Both of these behaviors are portrayed negatively as not tough or masculine enough. Finally, simply by seeking recognition and sympathy for his pain, Sam violated the masculine norm of enduring one's pain in silence.

Other athletes describe their attempts to earn the respect of other boys in high school by being ruthlessly aggressive both off and on the playing field.[7] Some of these players, like Sam, still were confronted with challenges about their masculinity when serious injuries interfered with their performance. A former high school athlete interviewed by Michael Messner said, "I was hurt, I couldn't play, and I got a lot of flack from everybody. The coach, you know: 'Are you faking it?' And I was in the whirlpool and [teammate] John came in and said, 'You fucking pussy!' I still remember that to this day. That hurt more than the injury. Later, people told me it was my fault because we lost, and I just couldn't handle that—not just coaches and other players, but people in the whole town . . . it hurts, it just really hurt."[8] Such negative references to women are commonly used to motivate male athletes to be more aggressive in every way by explicitly linking lack of aggressiveness with lack of masculinity.

Although coaches attempted to restrict physical combat to the playing field, this was somewhat problematic, since the boys themselves used fighting ability as an indicator of status among their peers.

At one point [during football practice] Hank suddenly started talking about somebody being a fag and how he hated him. He said, "I hate that guy; he's nothing but a faggot. I'd like to pop him one." Someone told him to be cool, the guy was not bothering him. Then Troy said, "Hey, you know you can beat the guy up, that's all that matters. Leave him alone. . . . Right after this Troy was talking to Mike and told him how he could beat him up because he was much tougher. A few minutes later, Troy was talking to another boy on the team, telling him that he could beat him up. He told him that he was overweight and he would get tired too fast in a fight. . . . I did notice a lot of personal-type confrontations such as that in football practice today, few of them serious. One of the reasons they weren't serious seemed to be that there was an acceptance of who actually was the toughest or the better fighter or who would win if there was a fight. Had there been ambiguity there, I believe that most of these episodes could have become hostile very quickly unless someone backed down. In that sense, it seems that the kids of Woodview do have a pecking order or a hierarchy based on physical toughness—specifically fighting ability—that if not rigid is at least recognized by many people in the hierarchy and outside the hierarchy. [Steve's notes]

Coaches tried to limit boys' battles to the playing field but were not always successful. Some boys refused to fight other boys at school for fear of having the coaches find out, but the verbal insults that followed their refusal just added to their anger and desire to respond antagonistically.

The guy at the table said that he would have punched the guy, but he didn't want the coach to find out. . . . Since he couldn't punch him, he walked away. When he did this, the other guy called him a puss, a weenie, and a chicken. This made him even angrier and he said he was really going to get that guy. [Steve's notes]

Many boys considered using physical force both off and on the playing field to deal with interpersonal conflicts. For example, one day Hank and Sam got upset with a boy over an incident on the bus. They tried to decide which of them was going to beat him up, since it was obvious that either of them could "whup" him, although it wasn't certain that he was "worth the effort."

Occasionally, a potential fight became a social event for a large number of students. For example, one day some boys reported that someone wanted to fight their friend Sam. While the boys and Sam agreed that Sam could beat this person up, there was concern that some big eighth-grade grits might join in. Sam's friends assured him that they would also join in and suggested possible matchups between boys on both sides that might occur, trying to convince Sam that they could handle his friends. When Sam did go outside accompanied by his friends they found a group of twenty-five to thirty kids standing in a circle.

> In the middle of the group was Ben, an eighth-grade grit. He was giving Sam a hard time about not fighting. He called him a pussy and kept pushing him in the arm. Sam said that they could call him whatever they wanted but he wasn't going to fight. The antagonism increased, and I was afraid that Sam was going to end up in a fight or worse, that we was going to start to cry. I was standing next to Hank, and he was real mad. He said he would be real glad when the eighth-graders were gone. He said they were always picking on people and that they made him sick. He said they were a bunch of jerks. [Steve's notes]

This example illustrates the pressure that boys are under to respond aggressively, even in the face of physical danger. It also shows that part of the training to be dominant consists of being subservient to those who have greater strength by virtue of their age and size. This sets up a pattern in which higher status is associated with intimidation of others and lower status is associated with submissive behavior.

Despite the numerous practices that emphasized the importance of being tough and aggressive, some boys continued to engage in behavior that other boys' viewed as inappropriate. This behavior was often the subject of indirect or direct ridicule. For example, one of the athletes rejected the hardened stance that most athletes took and developed a rather graceful, dancelike manner of walking and moving. One day after he had left the table, Hank referred to him as a "fagapolis." When Steve asked why he thought this, Hank said, "He just is. He's always doing faggy things."

Another boy in the school, who more obviously rejected the messages about stereotypical masculine behavior, spent little time around other boys, preferring the company of girls. Some days he was allowed to join the girls' groups without being ridiculed, but on other days some of the girls took advantage of his mild and ingratiating manner and bullied him into doing favors for them such as emptying their lunch trays. One time just his presence in the group provoked a series of insults.

> When Billy came over Sara got a malevolent expression
> on her face and yelled at him to go away because he was
> a faggot. She yelled at him that he's better leave Ted
> alone because she knew he was after Ted's body. This was
> very upsetting to Billy. He didn't even know who Ted
> was and got very confused, even blushed. The other girls,
> particularly Helen, picked up on this taunt and screamed
> in a very threatening manner to leave Ted's body alone,
> "You faggot!" They were just making this information up
> on the spot, I am sure, but Billy took their bluff seriously
> and was very upset by their threatening manner. For a
> while he looked like he was close to tears. What Billy did
> was hang in there though. He refused to go away.
> [Cathy's notes]

This boy showed no evidence of having a homosexual orientation, and in fact had crushes on some of the popular girls.

However, his very interest in associating with girls was a major deviation from the typical behavior of boys at this age and gave him isolate status in the school. Girls as well as boys used homosexual labels to challenge boys who failed to conform to more stereotypical masculine behavior.

In contrast to these examples, some boys found collective ways to challenge traditional expectations of being invincible and fearless. One group of boys shared an interest in baseball and often told stories about their experiences in various Little League games. We have already seen how the flexible nature of joint storytelling allowed boys to convey a wide range of concerns about issues such as toughness. This flexibility also provided them with opportunities to present counterviewpoints and thereby to challenge and detach from certain traditional expectations such as being a competent and fearless athlete. In the following story, Johnny starts by describing a large baseball pitcher who used to frighten him with his fast pitching.

Seventh Grade

JOHNNY: There's this big guy, against Triple Crown we were playin'—Triple Royal Crown last year—his name is Kevin Klinton 'n' he's about as big as Ken, 'n' he goes RRRRRROOOOMMM [Mimics throwing a wild ball] an' he throws mean. [Mimics throwing a wild ball again] He threw me a strike, then he goes sour 'n' he walked me. |I was lucky.

BOBBY: |Yeah. [Nods his head]

JOHNNY: He goes [Gestures] RRRROOOOOMMM and the ball goes WHOOOMMMM. [Mimics motion of whizzing ball with his hands] The guy's fast!

JOHNNY: [Pause] He's not really fast, he just scares you. He's so big and that little|

BOBBY: |He's huge man. [Shakes his head]

JOHNNY: Kevin Klinton, that little ball comes so|close
KEN: |Yeah.
[Bobby mimes huge pitcher winding up. Ken also mimes huge pitcher]

Instead of using narration to reinforce the concern with being stoic and fearless, Johnny uses narration here to re-create a situation in which he felt afraid. All of the comments and behaviors of other group members support the story Johnny is telling and the threatening nature of this large pitcher. In the process they are distancing themselves from the expectation that boys should be confident under all circumstances. Gary Fine also found that Little League players were sometimes criticized for expressing fear, but that once consensus emerged about a frightening event the expression of fear was seen as legitimate.[9] It is possible that certain athletic activities allow for a wider range of expressions of masculine behavior. Because baseball relies less on physical aggression than do either football or wrestling, it appears to promote a context for allowing the genuine expression of anxiety as well as encouraging a certain degree of competition.

In summary, while many of the messages about the nature of toughness were developed through the context of male athletic training in this school, the importance of being tough extended to behavior off the playing field as well as on it. Boys were continually challenged to develop more aspects of toughness, including the ability to deny pain and suppress feelings as well as respond combatively to verbal and physical attacks. Boys who rejected these messages were sometimes subject to ridicule by girls as well as boys, showing the difficulty boys faced when trying to escape the pressures of becoming masculine within this school setting. Through collaborative stories, however, some boys collectively detached themselves from these traditional concerns.

Ritual and Serious Insulting

A tough and competitive orientation was also an inherent part of insulting as practiced by the boys in most of the male groups. Boys typically displayed very little sensitivity to other boys' feelings during ritual insulting. It was generally each boy's responsibility to manage his own feelings.

Two main types of insulting have been identified. In one case, the initiator is required to use only insults the target would not perceive as being true and thus could easily respond to in a ritual manner.[10] In the other case, the initiator is free to use a range of insults and it is up to the respondent to *treat* the insult as if it isn't true, whether or not there is some truth in it.[11] Many Woodview boys practiced the latter form of insulting, in which the target was expected to keep his cool regardless of the type of insult received.

Boys who engaged in insulting often used it as a form of competition and as a means for directly comparing their insult skills with another boy. As long as new insults were introduced, the exchange continued. As soon as someone repeated an insult, the other boy would point this out and the exchange was over. If the quality or originality of the names decreased, the exchange ended. Sometimes there was a clear designated winner; at other times the outcome was ambiguous.

Some boys also used insulting as a means to enhance their status outside their own group. The highest-status boy in the seventh grade was known for his verbal aggressiveness.

Hank does seem to enjoy conflict or competition on a one-on-one basis. A couple of times today he left the table just to go down and abuse some kid at the end of the table, calling him a pud, a squirt, or a wimp. Then he would come back and tell the group how the guy had done nothing when he had said this. Hank would get a big smile on his face and was really pleased. [Steve's notes]

These cross-group insults posed much greater challenges than did within-group insulting. Because the insulter was not a friend, the meaning or intent of these insults was much more ambiguous. At the same time, a serious response could lead to a physical fight, something most boys would avoid engaging in with a higher-status group member. Thus, once a boy had gained a relatively high status within the school, he could more easily reinforce his status by insulting others.

Another way boys could win an insult exchange was by getting the other boy to lose his cool. Since being in control of one's emotions is an important aspect of toughness, becoming angry or upset by a peer's insult is a violation of the developing masculine norm.[12] Typically, if a boy responded emotionally to an initial insult, the exchange would immediately escalate to more serious insulting, as in the following example.

A little later on in lunch, Phil was called a vasectomy girl, a V.G., and then that was changed to a valley girl and then back to a vasectomy girl again. He took this very personally, and when it was done, he stood up and acted like he was going to be aggressive to whoever called him that. Jeff, Don, and Denny all took turns. They were somewhat scared of him in that they feared being hit by him, but at the same time, they were laughing and trying to keep their distance so that they could call him these names. . . . Most of the rest of the lunch was spent with the guys calling him these names and then running around the table. Don slid under the table whenever he gave chase and was taking spoonfuls of slush and throwing them at Phil from under the table. [Steve's notes]

Had Phil been able to respond initially by insulting back and not losing emotional control, this exchange might have continued as a ritual one. Once he responded personally, however, the attacks immediately escalated to a more serious level which in turn led to an even stronger response on his part. The physical chase returned the interaction to a more playful level, but Phil continued to be the target of the other members' playful attacks.

In rare cases, a boy would intervene in an insulting episode if he felt that an insult was unfair to another boy. In the following exchange, a basketball team member accused a member of a low-status group of not being good enough to have made the team. Immediately, a high-status group member intervenes, first by asking for a clarification and later by denying the validity of the challenge.

Seventh Grade
ERIC: [To Phil] Well, you're too sad to make that team, so you'll never know how wild it is.
MIKE: [To Phil] You gonna try out?
PHIL: No, I never tried out. [Elbows Eric lightly in the shoulder] You shut your mouth.
ERIC: You wouldn't have made it anyway.
MIKE: [To Eric] He probably could've.
ERIC: [To Mike] Who could he beat out?
MIKE: Jack Bonner.
ERIC: Huh uh. Jack can kick for a sixth-grader.
MIKE: I know, so he can have experience [unclear] that sucks man. He's never gonna play.

By intervening and later claiming that Eric probably could have made the team, Mike implied that these insults were unfair. At the same time, his intervention made it more difficult for Phil to make the insult exchange a ritual one. Instead of being able to respond immediately with a counterinsult, Phil ended up giving a serious response to Mike's question. Phil did try to put the interaction in a lighter mode by elbowing Eric and telling him to "shut your mouth," but after Mike's serious denial to Eric's next challenge the interaction moved into a serious debate about Phil's chances of having made the team.

Thus, through the common activity of insulting, boys receive additional messages about toughness. First, they are learning that they do not need to be responsible for the feelings of others since it is up to others to manage their own feelings. In addition, they are learning that insulting and even humiliating others is an acceptable means of gaining or demonstrating higher status. This was most evident in the behavior of boys toward isolates. Although girls also ridiculed isolates, they frequently were challenged or sanctioned by other girls for their insensitivity. Boys were more likely than girls to ridicule isolates and were never seen being sanctioned by their peers for doing so. In most cases, ridicule consisted of making fun of girls they thought were unattractive and/or overweight. They also ridiculed special education students, particularly girls, as in the following example.

> The tall special ed student sat at the end of our table by herself after getting her lunch. For about the next fifteen minutes, groups of two to five persons would go up to her and ask her questions or try to get her to say something that could be funny to the others around. Someone might point to another student in the cafeteria and ask her if she knew that he/she liked her. This would cause the student pointed out to act as if he/she had been poisoned and everyone could then laugh. I heard one boy repeatedly ask her if she knew what a homosexual was. He then volunteered a definition which included being a queer, a faggot, and a loony. The girl looked really shaken. [Steve's notes]

This painful episode shows the degree to which some boys have become insensitive to the feelings of others as well as the extent to which they have come to see the acceptability of ridiculing and humiliating low-status people. It is nowhere as extreme as the incident that occurred in Glen Ridge, New Jersey, in which a group of boys sexually abused and raped a retarded girl, but this and the example that follows show a similar tendency for particularly vulnerable students to become the victims of male aggression.

While most of the aggression aimed at isolates was in the form of verbal abuse, it could also include physical acts. In one case that Steve witnessed, a group of ten or twelve boys took turns trying to hit, kick, or otherwise physically harass a special education girl, while a group of about forty boys watched and encouraged them to continue. Although these boys are not encouraged within their peer groups or athletic teams to be sensitive to the feelings of people, it is still surprising that so many boys would participate in such an event.

Based on his experience in a boarding school, David Jackson gives an autobiographical account of why so many boys participate in verbal or physical abuse or fail to intervene despite their concern for the targets. "I couldn't afford to take Martin's side against the pack as I would have been turned on as well. To survive I had to keep silent *within* the pack. . . . It was painful to watch Martin writhing in embarrassed confusion but we knew if we didn't join in it would be our turn next."[13] This personal reflection further supports the link between ridicule and domination. Jackson, like many other boys, saw no option but to be either the dominator or the abused. To stop participating as a dominator or to intervene on the victim's behalf means becoming a potential victim of similar ridicule and harassment.

A closer examination of the practice of ritual insulting offers some explanation of why the messages regarding toughness were so strongly reinforced by male peers. Since the expected response is another insult rather than a denial or a challenge to the legitimacy of the first insult, this common routine offers boys few opportunities to challenge the content of insults. While a possible option to being called a "fag" or a "wimp" is to reply "So what?" or "Who cares?" these responses were extremely rare. Instead, by offering the typical response of a counterinsult, boys imply that they believe the content is negative but they are not taking it personally. In other words, they are not challenging the importance of being competitive, unemotional, aggressive, and heterosexual as they defend their own personal characters from charges of failing to measure up to these ideals.

In contrast to ritual insulting, collaborative storytelling was used by Woodview boys both to reinforce concerns about being tough and to offer counterviewpoints. The greater flexibility of this mode of talk meant that it could be used in a variety of ways. While some boys used this flexibility to illustrate the many dimensions of the concept of toughness, other boys used this same flexibility to create situations in which they could express some detachment from the expectation that they would be continually competent and fearless. Thus, at least one speech routine gave them an opportunity to express their resistance to the traditional expectations that were conveyed through other speech routines such as insult exchanges as well as through the explicit messages of athletic coaches.

In summary, boys in this school had numerous ways of reinforcing a competitive and aggressive orientation among their peers. Fundamental to this process was the legitimization of aggressive domination by school authorities within the context of sports. As Peter Lyman has noted, rule-governed aggression is useful to organizations because of the forceful energy it mobilizes.[14] In cases such as this, where winning is placed above the welfare of the opposing team members, teaching boys to be combative offers schools a competitive advantage. The coaches' attempts to channel the combativeness of these boys and limit it to the sports arena turned out to be ineffective, however. Since physical aggression was so highly valued within the team setting, it became one of the primary bases of informal status among the boys. It was also associated strongly with a masculine identity, so that avoidance of tough behavior could lead to challenges regarding one's masculinity. Verbal insulting itself became a source of peer status, in which causing others to lose their cool or be humiliated was an acceptable means of demonstrating superior status. Because Woodview's organized activities helped promote a highly stratified status system, boys were continually trying to demonstrate their superior status. As a result, even the high-status boys frequently engaged in verbal or physical aggression. At the same time, the isolates at Woodview were most at risk for verbal and, occasionally, physical abuse. Thus, the processes of maintaining a stereotypical masculine orientation were costly for many students.

This focus on toughness prevailed across social class boundaries. The highest-status group, which included several middle-class boys as well as some upper-working-class boys, saw itself as superior to other prep groups because of their greater toughness as well as their greater defiance of school rules. While the two medium-high-status groups engaged in much less insulting, they admired the toughness and defiance of the boys in the elite group. Some of the toughest behavior was found in boys from lower-working-class backgrounds who were in low-status groups, but they tended to be feared more than respected by their peers. Since many of these boys did not participate in school-sponsored sports or were unconcerned about being viewed positively by school officials, they did not gain status through the legitimization of toughness as the most popular boys did.

Other researchers have also demonstrated the way in which certain sports have become a central training ground for combative and even violent behavior. According to Michael Messner, "in many sports, achievement of goals (scoring and winning) is predicated on the successful utilization of violence—that is, these are activities in which the human body is routinely turned into a weapon to be used against other bodies, resulting in pain, serious injury, and even death."[15] Sports do not just reflect patterns of masculine aggression in society, but actively produce them. For example, Robert Connell and his colleagues explain how football teaches boys "drive" because "they are constantly running up against someone and have to overcome him in a test of personal superiority."[16]

Researchers who have examined the history of combat sports (that is, sports based on ritualized aggression) have found that they are strongly linked to patterns of male dominance. In the late 1800s and early 1900s, men responded to threats to male superiority by creating an exclusive cultural activity emphasizing physical strength.[17] Combat sports were justified partly as training grounds for war and partly as a means of developing "manliness"; they were introduced into schools to offset an environment that was perceived to be "overly feminized."[18] Initially, combat sports were especially popular in upper- and middle-class schools, where they were used to make up for a more general lack of emphasis on physical strength.[19] Now they are as important, if not more important, among working-class boys who, lacking other resources and choices, often perceive sports as the only legitimate context for establishing a masculine identity and a sense of self-worth.[20]

This focus on aggression in sports supports male dominance not just by excluding girls and women, but also by emphasizing and legitimizing physical strength as a means of overpowering others. Even men who are not athletes identify with those who are and see them as symbolic of male superiority. This is evident in the remarks of a man interviewed by Michael Messner. "A woman can do the same job as I can do—maybe even be my boss. But I'll be *damned* if she can go out on the field and take a hit from Ronnie Lott."[21] Even though most men do not have nearly the same physical capabilities as the athletes they admire, they nevertheless identify with the male power those athletes represent. As long as aggression and violence are legitimized in a society, the balance of power will favor men.[22]

Finally, it should be noted that not all boys and men benefit from this focus on male aggression as a form of superiority. Instead, the dominance of some men *depends* on the subordination of other men.[23] As we have clearly seen in this chapter, male aggression is often directed at other boys as well as at girls. In the next chapter, we will more carefully examine the way in which a focus on aggressive competition affects male-female relationships.

6

Crude Comments and Sexual Scripts

Many of the boys in this study were beginning to define themselves in relation to girls in the school or to girls more generally. We will see later that girls were developing a view of male-female relationships that both challenged and conformed to traditional heterosexual relationships. We saw fewer challenges to stereotypical notions on the part of boys, however. We also found that their shared orientation toward girls was primarily based on sexuality and that only a few boys admitted to having romantic or affectionate feelings toward girls.

Many studies have commented on the sexual (as opposed to romantic) focus of boys' orientation toward girls in adolescence. What was striking in our study was the *nature* of this sexual focus and the ways in which the boys were actively shaping each others' views about sexuality. It was clear that many boys began adolescence with a nonaggressive orientation toward sexuality that took the social context into account. In the following episode one of the most verbally aggressive boys in the school, Hank, reveals some sensitivity to the importance of situational factors when discussing sexuality. However, the pressures to be sexually active and competitive transform his orientation into a much more impersonal one.

> Sam was acting as a messenger from Hank to the girls. They wanted him to come down to their group, but he didn't want to. Joe told Hank that he was crazy not to; that she [Cindy] might want to fuck him on the other side of the school. Hank said he [Joe] was stupid; that wasn't going to happen and that nothing was going to happen. He added that it might if they were alone, but not with everyone around. Someone said that he didn't know how and didn't even want to fuck her. Hank got mad and said, "I'll fuck her anytime—right here, right now, any time, anyplace." [Steve's notes]

At first Hank indicated that the public setting of the school is not appropriate for sexual intercourse. After someone challenged his sexual abilities and interests, he moved to a much more impersonal and aggressive stance regarding sexuality, where timing and location become irrelevant. Since Hank had a reputation for being tough and competitive, it is not surprising that he responded so strongly when accused of lacking sexual knowledge and interest. It is likely that Hank's reaction was based largely on fear of losing status among his peers. This illustrates the way in which even boys who may appear to be inherently aggressive are influenced to become even more aggressive, in this case in the sexual arena, through insults and challenges from peers.

These boys' view of sexuality is clearly being shaped by their more general view that boys should be tough and domineering. The sensitivity Hank initially demonstrated was replaced by a much more impersonal stance toward sexuality, one in which the feelings of girls are disregarded in the attempt to demonstrate one's sexual prowess and aggressiveness. This corresponds with the general competitive orientation of "winning at all costs." It also reflects the perceived lack of need to be sensitive to other people's feelings. Now this attitude is being transferred to boys' newly developing relationships with girls.

Boys were also expected to defend their "sexual property" aggressively. This further reflects the tendency to define sexual activity as another type of rivalry in which boys compete with other boys for conquests. Within this framework it is acceptable for boys to make sexual advances toward other boys' girlfriends, since it is up to the boys whose "property" has been invaded to defend their territory. In the following episode, a boy who fails to stand up to a competitor is negatively evaluated by his peers.

> Perry and Richard walked over behind Tammy, and Perry acted like he was grabbing her bottom. Richard went ahead and actually did it. She turned around, but didn't retaliate in any way. They came back over to the table and retold what had happened. The point they stressed was that Carl (who was going with Tammy) was standing there when they grabbed her. After Richard grabbed her, Carl took a step toward Richard and said his name. Richard stuck his chest forward and said, "What?" Carl just backed down. Consensus was that Carl was a pussy. Hank and Joe were the most outspoken about this. [Steve's notes]

Even though Carl made some initial attempt to defend his girlfriend from unwelcome sexual advances, he was criticized for not continuing to stand up to a possible confrontation with Richard. At the same time, Richard was not criticized for making a sexual advance toward someone else's girlfriend. These responses

85

support sexual prerogative and promiscuity for boys, while re-inforcing a view that girls are sexual objects to be fought over. The responses also illustrate how girls are viewed as territorial property to be violated when challenging another boy's masculinity.

These boys appear to be applying the standards of aggressiveness and competition which they have learned to their newly formed relationships with girls. Studies of older male athletes and fraternity members found that women were often referred to as objects of sexual conquests and were the targets of antagonistic sexual jokes.[1] Apparently this competitive, conquest orientation toward women continues to be the main orientation for many older male athletes and fraternity men. As girls and women are increasingly forced into the narrow, male-defined role of objects to be conquered and boasted about, they are at considerable risk of being the targets of displaced male aggression.[2]

Sexual Teasing

As mentioned previously, boys are expected to demonstrate their masculinity by controlling their emotions during insult exchanges. According to Peter Lyman, sexual teasing is also part of learning to keep one's cool.[3] Many of the boys in this study had learned how to keep their cool during insult exchanges, but few were able to control their anger over sexual teasing.

Teasing routines were typically more flexible than insult exchanges: teasing involved a much wider range of playful behavior, including mock threats, mock challenges, and imitations of verbal and nonverbal behavior. As with ritual insulting, the nature of the response to a teasing comment played a critical role in determining whether a playful tone was maintained.[4] There was a wider range of possible responses, from joking denials to self-mocking remarks, but the greater flexibility of teasing routines, as well as their less competitive structure, may have made it difficult for boys to know how to respond to their peers' teasing comments. Thus, in many cases boys responded to such remarks by getting angry and/or leaving the interaction.

> Kevin and Tom were both giving Mike a hard time about Patty wanting to go with Mike. He denied it, but he wasn't very convincing. Kevin said that he knew he was interested because he saw him grabbing her tits in the hall. Mike called him a liar, but Kevin and others just laughed and Kevin imitated Patty saying, "Oh Mike, don't leave. Stay with me and I'll let you do anything." Mike looked angry and walked away. [Steve's notes]

While overtly sexual teasing was most common, boys were also sensitive to being teased about their romantic interest in girls, especially if it included letting the girl involved know of their interest.

> Joe and Hank were asking Sam if he really liked some girl. I asked who it was and Eric told me I didn't want to know, insinuating that she was ugly. Sam denied all of this. Then Joe and Hank left the table to tell her that Sam liked her. This upset Sam, who called them assholes and said he was going to kick their butts. Joe ignored it, and Hank told him he could try if he wanted to. Later Sam was eating by himself at a table, and Joe asked why. Hank said it was because he was pissed about the girl. Sam said it was only because he was hungry and decided to get something to eat. Joe said, "Aah, poor Sam. Eating by himself cause his friends did him wrong." Then Hank and Joe sighed together a couple of times in fake sympathy. Sam acted like he didn't notice any of their actions. [Steve's notes]

While girls relied on empathy to limit the extent of unpleasant teasing, most boys appeared to believe that it was up to the target of the teasing to manage any unpleasant feeling that arose. Although Sam tried to let his friends know that they had taken the teasing too far, they ignored his physical threats and made fun of him for being so upset that he needed to isolate himself from the group. Again, the orientation toward "being tough" and "keeping one's cool" prevailed.

At times boys also made sexually teasing and insulting comments directly to girls. These comments implied that the only interest they or their friends had in girls was as sexual objects.

> Cindy came over to the table and wanted to know who was throwing stuff. She addressed herself to Eric. Eric grabbed her arms when she got close. Joe told her that he wanted to eat her and grabbed her waist. She told him to let go. Joe said he changed his mind and walked away. Eric started pulling her down on his lap and told her, "Just a little more. I can almost see down your shirt." She got away, and, before she attacked Eric, Bobby called her over and started talking to her. She calmed down immediately. [Steve's notes]

Through their aggressive sexual comments and behaviors, these boys displayed their group's increasingly aggressive stance toward sexuality. These behaviors appeared to anger Cindy, who was about to respond by confronting Eric. Just at this point, a boy from a different peer group intervened and kept the interaction from escalating.

Barrie Thorne found that the elementary students in her study often had different interpretations of the same male-female interaction. What girls defined as a serious violation, boys often viewed as "just playing." It is likely that Cindy's view of Eric and Joe's behavior differed significantly from their view of it as "playful, harmless behavior." As Thorne notes, these differences persist—adult men and women often disagree about what should be viewed as sexual harassment and/or abuse.[5]

Sometimes the aggressive sexual stance demonstrated by boys made the targets so angry that potential romantic connections were broken. For example, one day a boy prevented a girl from responding to his friend's request to "go with him" by treating her as a sexual object.

> She [Tammy] stopped at our group to say "hi" and waited until Richard said "hi" as well. She stood there smiling, and finally Richard said, "Well, what do you say—yes or no? Are you going to go with me? Come on and go with me." Sam then said, "Yeah, go with him. He just wants some." Tammy got mad and tried to hit Sam saying, "I'll give you some." She then turned and walked away from the group. Richard never got his answer. [Steve's notes]

Tammy offered a very effective response to Sam's sexual reference to Richard "wanting some" by transforming the meaning of "some" to her physical attack on Sam. However, while Tammy clearly let Sam know his comment made her angry, none of the boys, including Richard, sanctioned Sam's behavior. Instead, Richard missed out on an opportunity to form a relationship with Tammy, largely because his group's approach to sexuality was one that is alienating to most girls.[6]

In his study of fraternities, Lyman found that some men thought that sexual jokes are vulgar but necessary for strengthening male bonds. They did, however, feel it was a mistake to reveal their "crudeness" to women, since they did not think women were as accustomed to such lewd remarks. However, many sexual jokes and comments about girls and women such as those described here are not only lewd but also sexually oppressive in that they portray females as passive objects of male sexual desire and aggression.[7]

Occasionally, boys in the school commented on the crude or "gross" nature of another boy's remark. Since boys did not believe that others should limit their teasing or insulting remarks, the comments seldom had any effect on their behavior, as the next episode illustrates.

> Kevin, Bobby, and Johnny were on one side of the group. Bobby got the attention of a girl who was sitting in another part of the cafeteria. When she looked at him, he said that Kevin liked her and wanted to get to know her. Kevin just ducked down so that he couldn't be seen. . . . Bobby kept this up and Johnny joined in. Then Joe joined in, saying "He likes you and wants your body. He wants your ass." Kevin said that was gross. Joe continued telling her that Kevin "wanted to put his prick up her shithole." Bobby and Johnny stopped talking to the girl at this point. I don't think they wanted to be connected with Joe's comments. Joe turned to Eric and asked if he had heard him. Eric said no and Joe repeated it. [Steve's notes]

Joe appears to have used this interaction as an opportunity to show off his ability to make crude and aggressive sexual comments to a girl, since he made a point of reporting his behavior to Eric. He was not willing to modify his behavior when Kevin told him he was being "gross," because he apparently saw more advantage in impressing other boys with the extent of his grossness. In this case, the girl was reduced to an object through which Joe could display his sexually aggressive stance. Because Joe's comments depersonalized Kevin as well the girl he was interested in and reduced the chances of a relationship starting, it is evident that boys as well as girls can be the victims of dominant boys' aggressive talk. Also, since Joe's behavior was unaffected by Kevin's sanction, the only option left for boys who have negative reactions to sexually aggressive talk is to distance themselves from the interaction.

In his study of older athletes, Michael Messner also found that some disapproved of the way girls were treated like objects, judged by their appearance, and spoken about in abusive language. Rather than trying to voice their complaints about these behaviors to the boys involved, however, they distanced themselves more from the jock culture during their later years in high school.[8] Again, the norms against setting limits on dominant boys' verbal behavior appear to be so strong that those boys who do object to the treatment of girls usually remain silent. Also, given the power of these norms, a boy would need to have extremely high status within a peer group in order to be able to challenge them successfully.[9]

Girls as Teasers and Insulters

Boys tended to take the initiative in incidents of cross-sex insulting, but occasionally boys who were the only male members of girls' groups found themselves the targets of sexual teasing or insulting. Since teasing typically consisted of mocking comments, whether threats, challenges, or other remarks, girls frequently used teasing to make fun of traditional images of romantic and/or sexual relationships. Thus, just as collaborative storytelling was sometimes used by boys to resist traditional gender messages, girls frequently used teasing as a collective means for expressing resistance of and detachment from traditional roles. For example, one day several girls developed an extensive teasing episode based on the imaginary fatherhood of a male friend.

The major joke that came up this period was that Laura had gotten pregnant and that Jerry was the father. All the girls kept saying this loudly and laughing about the idea. Some of them told Jerry. He yelled down toward them, asking them to clarify what they were saying about Laura. They said, "Laura's pregnant." Then he asked who they were saying was the father. They told him, "It's you; you are the father." Jerry immediately turned red and his eyes got bigger, though he was giggling. He said it wasn't true and was laughing as he did because the idea was such a ridiculous one. Given Jerry's small size, he obviously hasn't entered into puberty yet. Laura is rather tall and hefty and definitely looks several years older than Jerry. Then Laura came over and sat by Jerry. She teased him, too, by saying that everyone was embarrassing Jerry and that they should leave him alone. She grabbed him in a rather rough, yet teasing, manner as she said this. Everyone was laughing a lot. A male teacher came by and asked Jerry, "What kind of trouble are you causing this time?" Several girls told him that "He got Laura pregnant." The teacher opened his mouth and pretended to be shocked. This made everybody laugh louder and made Jerry blush. [Cathy's notes]

Immediately after this episode, Laura took Jerry by the hand and pretended to be his mother, dragging him around as she might a small child, first jerking him in one direction and then in another. They continued to find amusement in this gender reversal, as did their peers.

In this case, the peer group used teasing to mock traditional sexual relationships by pretending that an older and larger girl has been sexually involved with a small boy. Following this scenario with a contrasting one—that of a mother with a small boy—underscores the mockery of the first scenario. Also, because it is clear that the girl has a greater power advantage in the mother role-play, the coupling of these two scenarios allows the girls to create an even safer context for experimenting with future male-female sexual roles.

In contrast to teasing, the sexual insults that girls directed toward boys were more likely to reinforce stereotypical gender concerns. As shown previously, girls as well as boys used homosexual labels to insult boys who did not appear to be tough or who spent time with girls rather than with their male peers. They also insulted boys by referring to their sexual inadequacy, including the small size of their genitals, as in the following example.

> Paul mentioned getting hit somewhere twice before today and Ali said, "Oh do you have anything worth getting hurt?" Ali thought this was really funny and repeated the episode to both me and to Patty. Paul was sort of embarrassed about this. Later on she said something else to him, and he said, "Oh, you've gone too far now." [Donna's notes]

It was ironic that even the boys whose company and attention the girls liked were at times insulted for the very behavior of sitting with them. In the following episode, Natalie initiated an insult exchange with Jimmy, a boy she was coupled with for a short time several weeks previously and would like to go with again. Several of the other girls in the group also liked this boy and had been playfully teasing him during much of the lunch period. While the flexibility of teasing routines easily allowed for many group members to join in, these girls found a way to make ritual insulting a more collaborative endeavor, with several girls constructing the insults aimed indirectly or directly at Jimmy.

Eighth Grade
NATALIE: How come he don't ruin your family life—is he sterile?

93

ELLEN: No, we was t— [Ellen breaks into laughter before finishing her sentence. Everyone else laughs too.]

NATALIE: Well? [Giggles]

GWEN: I don't know, ask him.

NATALIE: Jimmy, do you feel weird sittin' around with a bunch of girls?

ELLEN: Well, he's never gotten me pregnant yet so maybe he is.

RHODA[?]:   No, he feels right at home. [Sentence less audible]

NATALIE: Okay, but

ELLEN: ˙   Natalie.

NATALIE: *Why?* You're around your own kind.

GWEN: He likes it. [Ellen and Rhoda repeatedly try to get Natalie's attention by saying her name.]

JIMMY: [to Natalie] Huh?

TRICIA: That's an insult. [There is a brief side conversation between Rhoda and Natalie.]

JIMMY: That would make you guys bad.

This insulting exchange was transformed into a collaborative activity by Natalie's first insult concerning Jimmy's sexual inadequacy, in the form of a question addressed to both Ellen and Gwen rather than being addressed directly to Jimmy. Before Ellen could finish her response, Natalie offered a second insult, this time about the weirdness of Jimmy's association with girls. Although this second insult was in the form of a question addressed to Jimmy, it was also responded to and expanded upon by other girls, including the questioner herself. All of the comments serve to further develop the theme of association with girls, saying "he feels right at home," that "you're around your own kind," and that "he likes it." Jimmy eventually offered a counterinsult, "that would make you guys bad," implying that they have incriminated themselves by claiming he is around his own kind. This insult turns the theme of similarity away from gender to being "bad," thus casting everyone into a deviant role.

This particular insult exchange is important in that it shows the creative way adolescents can alter the structure of insulting from a one-on-one duel to a more collaborative endeavor, with several girls uniting against one boy. The basic structure of responding to an insult with a counterinsult still remains, however, and thus this exchange serves to convey rather than challenge the message that there is something wrong with not always being sexually potent or with a boy choosing the company of girls.

It is somewhat surprising that girls would insult boys (especially boys they like) about spending time with girls. However, girls and boys seem to have some awareness of each others' main concerns and use these as the basis for their insults. Thus, girls as well as boys often fail to reflect on the messages implicit in the content of standard insults and therefore help to maintain the negative orientation toward girls that is a central aspect of some male peer cultures. In addition, they are reinforcing boys' concerns with heterosexuality and sexual performance in relationships with girls. By encouraging boys to avoid informal contact with girls and to prove themselves sexually, girls are negating the value of female companionship and reinforcing the primacy of boys as sexual actors. This shows that both girls and boys contribute to maintaining beliefs about male-female relationships that ultimately limit the options for everyone.

Movies and Other Sexual Scripts

Many of the boys in Woodview had much less contact with girls than the boys in the high-status group did. A few of the boys in one of the groups that sat on the low-status side of the cafeteria occasionally had girlfriends; others had never had a girlfriend. The boys in some of these groups relied extensively on the media for developing a shared understanding of male sexuality. Movies shown on cable television were a resource for storytelling and skit reenactment among this group of boys.[10] They provided them with a common experience to use as the basis for collaborative talk, since they did not engage in athletic activities together. The boys generally selected scenes that had some sexual and/or violent activity to reenact for their collaborative skits, as in the following example. They had been reenacting other sexual scenes from the movie *Quest for Fire* when Jack brought up this particular scene.

Eighth Grade

JEFF: An' the very first one |

TODD: | Nude girl was bent over by the creek man. He comes along and sits down on the bank man and goes [Briefly gyrates hips, then sits down] [Laughter]

JEFF: He was—he was the lookout, an' he was lookin' out.

MACK: Together.

WALTER: He was lookin' around an' all of a sudden these three girls are drinkin' [Mimes girls drinking water from their hands]

JEFF: He goes da dum da dum da dum [Mimes running] "Oh! Oh! Oh!" [Gyrates, imitating copulation, then sits down] He grabs 'em by the shoulders [Holds out arms and convulses his body] "Ooh! Ooh! Ooh! Ooh!"

WALTER: An' the best thing about it is she just sits there [Mimes girls drinking from hands] an' drinks while she's getting hosed man. [Giggling]

JEFF: She jumps—she jumps an' then [Mimes drinking from hands; Mack also mimes drinking.]

The content of the scene being described conveys the message that men are active sexually and that the only sexual role of women is to be the target for men's sexual urges. This movie, which is about early human behavior, includes no dialogue, so the entire interaction between the man and woman in this scene consists of his matter-of-fact use of her body. These boys found this type of interaction exciting, and by describing it they were both creating and reinforcing a view that sexual aggressiveness is an essential aspect of masculinity. It is the film's depiction of women they found most attractive, however. As Walter commented at one point, the best thing about this scene is the woman's passive response and the fact that she continues to drink water while they are having intercourse. This impression of women having no sexual desires and of passively submitting to male sexual prerogative is reinforced by Walter's interpretation of and commentary on this scene.

In a more extensive analysis of adolescent boys' interpretation and use of movies in their peer culture, Melissa Milkie found that they often focus on scenes of sexual domination and emphasize the theme of sexual aggression in their interpretations. Even if the movie has many other more highly developed themes, they ignore them in favor of the scenes that show sexual and/or violent behavior.[11] Thus, boys are actively selecting aspects of adult culture that have salience for their future lives. At the same time, in order to participate successfully in collaborative reenactments of movie scenes with their peers, they need to focus their attention selectively on sexual scenes when watching movies.

Milkie also found that adolescent boys strongly identify with the men in these movies.[12] While acting out the scenes, they are imagining themselves either as being the sexual initiator or as encouraging the male actor in his sexual exploits, as is obvious in the following reenactment from *History of the World—Part One*.

Eighth Grade
WALTER: That was . . . how about when he didn't
know—he goes—she goes [Mimes taking off a shirt]
"Take me," an' I go "Yeah!" [Giggles]
JEFF: Man, did you see that one thing—it was [Cupping
his hands at his chest] an' was [Indicating a large bust]
WALTER: [Indicating cleavage] Yeah, up an' out. I go
"God! Get her!"

These scripts follow what Victor Seidler claims is a key fantasy
of many men—having women meet their sexual needs. In such a
fantasy men do not need to take responsibility for stating their
needs, nor do they need to be able to negotiate others' needs.[13]

This theme of men as sexual actors in contrast to women as
passive sexual objects came up in other collaborative stories in
this group. Some of their tales about adult women in their lives
mingled fact with fantasy and included fantasized sexual behavior on their part, as in the following episode.

Eighth Grade
JACK: You know, the bus driver, she never wears a bra
man, and she goes over a bump and her tits go [Bounces
in his chair] ooblablabla, an' she's wearin' this loose
sweater |
WALTER: |Yeah, [Bouncin' his head] there's a lady sittin'
next to you an' your head goes and she goes "What are
you doing?" an' I go [Bouncing his head and sticking out
his tongue] "Nothing." [Bounce, bounce] "Nothing."
JEFF: Loose sweater—she had a loose sweater on, an' we
went over a bump an' then all of a sudden one of them
nipples popped out [Mimes nipple popping out] an' I go
wow. I'm rolling around dyin' laughin' man, man. [Tips
his chair back] [Scott falls over on the table laughing, slapping the table.] [Laughter]

MACK: [Pulls out the front of his shirt] Boing!

WALTER: [Pulls out the front of his shirt] Wooow!

Again, this story is one in which a woman is portrayed as the object of male sexual desire and curiosity. Walter was fantasizing about being able to act on this desire, while having another woman remain oblivious to his action. Possibly the imagined passivity of women decreases the fear these boys may have regarding actual sexual encounters, since they themselves have had little interaction with girls in the school. Also, since the media focus much more on women as sexual objects than as sexual actors, it is not surprising that these boys have incorporated such a view and continue to strengthen it through their collaborative stories.

Unlike the examples given in chapter 5, where joint story-telling was occasionally used by boys collectively to resist traditional messages, these examples show boys primarily using collaborative stories to incorporate and convey more stereotypical masculine themes of sexual domination. Sexual insults were also used by both boys and girls to convey traditional concerns. This may be largely due to the very structure of such routines, which offer few opportunities for mocking stereotypical roles.

A Culture of Sexual Aggression

Thus, many boys were developing a view of girls as sexual objects, not sexual actors. To the extent that girls become objectified, it is even easier to discount their feelings, including possible feelings of discomfort and humiliation. It is important to note that boys with very high status as well as those with low status developed this orientation toward girls. This finding seems to contrast with research on working-class Chicano men, which has claimed that negative views toward women and a machismo view of men are due largely to channeling social class conflict into the arena of gender.[14] If sexual aggression toward women is due only to suppressed anger from being at the bottom of a social hierarchy, we would expect to see such behavior predominantly on the part of the lower-status boys and men.

Instead, it appears that when toughness and competition are valued, boys and men at high as well as low status levels are encouraged by some of their peers to approach male-female relations competitively and/or aggressively. According to Victor Seidler, having sex is a way of proving one's masculinity. For many men, sex becomes another form of achievement as well as a way to assert power over women. Furthermore, Seidler claims that masculinity must continually be proven, since it relies on external validation rather than an inner sense of self. Thus, even high-status men might feel a need to prove their masculinity continually by having new sexual conquests.[15]

All these informal activities create taken-for-granted notions about male sexuality. Because the activities themselves are so routine, the messages they convey are often viewed as being "natural" or "typical" orientations toward sexuality and are seldom challenged. The only evidence of collective challenges we saw at Woodview was through the teasing routines initiated by girls, who used the mocking nature of this activity to make fun of stereotypical male-female sexual roles. While boys in the medium-high-status groups were much less likely than those in higher- or lower-status groups to engage in aggressive sexual behavior and, in general, were more sensitive to girls' concerns, they found few successful ways to challenge the sexist behaviors of their peers. On occasion they were berated for not being more aggressive in defending their "sexual property," and when their attempts to curtail the crude remarks of other boys proved ineffective, they tended to distance themselves from such behavior by sitting apart from them rather than persist in trying to stop it. At this age, at least, it appears that boys have few opportunities to effectively challenge messages regarding male sexuality as another arena for competition.

Only recently have researchers begun to identify these and similar behaviors in school settings from elementary to college level as being part of a culture of rape and sexual aggression. Nan Stein found that sexual harassment is a frequent public occurrence in elementary and secondary schools across the country, in small towns and large cities alike. "Examples of sexual harassment that happen in public include attempts to snap bras, grope at girls' bodies, pull down gym shorts, or flip up skirts; circulating 'summa cum slutty' or 'piece of ass of the week' lists; designating special weeks for 'grabbing the private parts of girls'; nasty, personalized graffiti written on bathroom walls; sexualized jokes, taunts, and skits that mock girls' bodies, performed at school-sponsored pep rallies, assemblies, or halftime performances during sporting events; and outright physical assault and even rape in school."[16] Like our findings, which link sexual aggression to other forms of aggressive behavior within the school environment, Stein sees these acts of sexual harassment as an extension of bullying behavior in which boys as well as girls are targets.

The girls Stein studied report having few effective strategies for dealing with sexual harassment. Their own attempts to end it are often unsuccessful, and adults often fail to take the problem seriously, or else ignore it altogether. As one fifteen-year-old wrote, "It was like fighting an invisible, invincible enemy alone. I didn't have a clue as to what to do to stop it, so I experimented [with] different approaches. Ignoring it only made it worse. It made it easier for them to do it, so they did it more. Laughing at the perpetrators during the assaults didn't dent the problem at all, and soon my friends became tired of doing this. They thought it was a game. Finally I wrote them threatening letters. This got me in trouble. But perhaps it did work. I told the school administrators what had been happening to me. They didn't seem to think it a big deal, but they did talk to the three biggest perpetrators. The boys ignored the administrators and it continued. And they were even worse."[17] Faced with little official response to this problem and limited options for dealing with it, girls as young as fourteen become resigned to sexual harassment. "I felt like the teacher (who was a man) betrayed me and thought I was making a big deal out of nothing. But most of all, I felt really bad about myself because it made me feel slutty and cheap. It made me feel mad too because we shouldn't have to put up with that stuff, but no one will do anything to stop it. Now sexual harassment doesn't bother me as much because it happens so much it almost seems normal. I know that sounds awful, but the longer it goes on without anyone doing anything, the more I think of it as just one of those things that I have to put up with."[18]

Recent studies at the college level reveal the extent to which this sexual competition is taken within many fraternities.[19] There, sexual success not only includes having multiple sexual partners, but also getting women to do things they don't want to do and to perform sexual acts that the men consider demeaning, such as fellatio and anal intercourse. It can also include telling stories about the most disgusting and/or humorous sexual experiences they have had, further distancing themselves from intimacy with women. "Sex as a competitive arena necessarily results in exploiting girls and women, because the motive is to 'score,' to impress one's male friends rather than to relate to the female."[20] Those fraternity men who do treat women with respect and do not take advantage of them are often berated by their brothers for not "sharing" the opportunity to exploit a vulnerable woman.

We believe it is time for school officials and all concerned adults to take this culture of rape and sexual aggression more seriously. Given the high rate of sexual violence toward young women, it appears that the occurrence of such violence, not just our awareness of it, has increased.[21]

7

Learning to Smile Through the Pain

A major focus of being female at Woodview was a focus on attractiveness. This has long been part of the construction of femininity in most Western cultures.[1] Increasing attention has been brought to the nature of this appearance preoccupation among American women and the way it prevents them from focusing on more constructive aspects of themselves, such as who they are or what they are capable of accomplishing.[2] It is becoming more and more clear that this is one of the main areas in which women are hindered by stereotypical notions of femininity.

At Woodview, concerns about attractiveness were promoted primarily through the high-status activity of cheerleading. This focus was most evident during the actual cheerleading tryouts. Although school officials attempted to professionalize the selection of new cheerleaders by including cheerleaders and secondary teachers as judges, it was clear that appearance continued to be an important selection criterion. The teacher who organized the tryouts told the judges to keep it in mind as they selected the candidates.

> She also told them to pay attention to the person's weight, saying, "If you don't like the way they look, you wouldn't like them to stand in front of you." [Donna's notes]

This message conveys the essence of cheerleaders as adornments to a team as well as promoters of team enthusiasm and support. The fact that cheerleaders are seen as team representatives makes their appearance salient in the context of a culture that places a high value on female beauty. To be the best representatives, they should be highly attractive as well as capable of promoting school spirit.

Officially, appearance was included in the judging of cheerleaders under the category of "sparkle." Ten of the fifty total points a candidate could obtain were allotted to this category, as the cheerleading coach explained to the candidates during one of the practice sessions prior to the tryouts.

> At one point, Mrs. Tolson started to tell them what they were going to be judged on, saying they would get ten points for sparkle, which was their smile, personality, bubbliness, appearance, attractiveness—not that all cheerleaders had to be attractive, but it was important to have a clean appearance, not to be sloppy, have messy or greasy hair, because that doesn't look like a cheerleader. [Donna's notes]

Although appearance was one of the official categories, there was some attempt to downplay its importance when talking with the candidates. This was because the coach received several complaints from parents whose daughters felt they needed new clothes for the cheerleading tryouts. To take the focus off enhancing attractiveness through one's dress, the coach instead emphasized neatness. Throughout the practice sessions girls were reminded to wear a clean, neat outfit for tryouts and to have clean, neatly combed hair. This emphasis on neatness continued despite the physical nature of this activity, which includes cartwheels and backflips. It was important to have the skills to do these gymnastic routines, but it was equally important to find ways to maintain a neat, feminine appearance throughout the performance. This again conveys the message to girls that how they look is as important as what they do.

Another way in which cheerleading candidates were encouraged to enhance their looks was by remembering to smile. Smiling was considered an important part of the cheerleading role—something that made you "look like a cheerleader." Girls were encouraged to smile to cover up feelings that might accompany their efforts, such as pain and concentration.

> When they were doing a stunt, she [the coach] said she wanted them to smile through the pain. Later on, when they were practicing the stunts in front of the eighth-graders, Karla [an eighth-grade cheerleader] continually reminded them to smile as they were working on their jumps. The way Karla put it was, "Smile the whole time." And at the end of one cheer, Mrs. Tolson said, "Smile, my gosh!" because they had looked particularly serious. [Donna's notes]

The need to remind the girls to smile throughout the practices indicates that it took considerable effort to mask other feelings. When told she was not smiling, one candidate said she was too nervous. However, conveying nervousness, pain, or concentration, rather than peppy enthusiasm greatly diminished the extent to which these girls portrayed a cheerleading image, and thus decreased their chance of succeeding in the tryouts.

The judges themselves evaluated the candidates' appearance during the decision-making process. Both neatness and cuteness were mentioned, as were the quality of their smiles. For example, one judge noted that the girl they were discussing had a cute smile. Another judge disagreed, indicating through imitation that the girl's smile was forced. This judge rated her more negatively than did the first one. Although weight was taken into account, one year some girls who were considered overweight were selected. The judges suggested that they be put on diets, preserving the idea that thinness is an important aspect of cheerleaders' appearance.

In contrast, no emphasis was placed on appearance by the female athletic coaches at Woodview. Instead, athletic activity was considered one area where you did not have to be very concerned about your appearance. Girls who wore new, coordinated sweatsuits to practice were mocked by other girls with comments like, "Don't you look cute today"; one girl who was obviously concerned about having boys see her in her volleyball uniform was told by a teammate, "No one cares what you look like. I sure don't."

Nonetheless, appearance was not entirely irrelevant to female athletes. During gymnastics competitions, the few male students who attended spent much of their time criticizing the appearance of various gymnasts. In her study of high school athletes, Janet Enke found that female team members also informally evaluated the attractiveness rather than the athletic abilities of their opponents.[3]

Schools such as Woodview officially promote a concern with appearance primarily through cheerleading, and the prestige given to cheerleading increases its importance in other school-sponsored activities. For example, cheerleaders who are also athletes bring the status of their greater visibility as cheerleaders and their attractiveness into the athletic setting, often disrupting a team's focus on achievement.[4] In addition, the high profile given to cheerleading means that traits that are valued in cheerleaders also have a greater impact on the school's informal peer culture.

Boys' Focus on Girls' Appearance in Peer Interaction

Many Woodview boys focused their evaluation of girls on their attractiveness. In fact, male interest in their bodies as being sexual and appealing could arouse the deepest level of appearance anxiety in girls. For example, one day a group of eighth-grade girls discussed a male ranking of female peers.

> Penny said that she had seen a list some boys had made which rated girls in the class. Karla was at the top, then Sara, then Peggy or Darlene. They said that they had told these guys, "Thanks a lot" for not including them on the list. Bonnie said, "Did you notice that all of those girls are early figure people?" indicating that the reason she thought they were rated highly was because they have a figure already. Then they pointed to Sara and said, "There she is. She's the one with the big hips. You can't miss her." [Donna's notes]

While these girls tried to attribute the greater perceived attractiveness of other girls to their early development of breasts and broader hips, implying that their own development was on a more normal schedule, they were definitely being influenced by the power of male gaze. Informal rankings such as this remind girls that they are being evaluated on a daily basis, even when they haven't entered formal beauty contests or cheerleading tryouts.

Boys frequently referred to the physical appearance of girls they knew, both in their presence and when the girls were absent. For example, one day a boy announced at lunch, "Any girl who thinks she's beautiful, stand up." The appearance of someone's girlfriend was a typical topic of conversation, usually implying that some feature of hers was unattractive or that she was ugly in general. Even some of the prettiest girls in the school, cheerleaders and other high-status-group members, were criticized by boys for having ugly faces or deficient bodies. Barrie Thorne found that some college students remembered being teased by boys for having large breasts, while others reported being teased for having small breasts.[5] This again points to the fact that few, if any, girls have bodies that are not subject to male evaluation.

The boys' appearance was not irrelevant to girls, but rather than discuss the minor flaws of their respective boyfriends they tended to talk more about the few boys they felt were at the extremely low end of the attractiveness scale.

> They were talking about Don. Ellen said, "Don is gross. He's really ugly." Then she laughed and said, "Rhoda's going with him." I think they said he was tall and had greasy hair. Then Beckie started asking, "Is he worse than so-and-so?" and Ellen would answer yes. She named a couple of people, and Don came out on the low end each time. But then Tricia asked, "Who's worse, Don or Roger?" They laughingly agreed that Roger is the worst." [Stephanie's notes]

Thus, while boys were scrutinizing the flaws of even the most attractive girls in the school, girls tended simply to avoid being associated with boys that their peers considered "real losers."

108

The Role of Girls' Gossip

Even when girls are by themselves, their conversations are often dominated by cultural standards and male perspectives that highlight the importance of good looks. Girls themselves contribute to this, especially through gossip about the looks and dress of other girls. When we first told students we were interested in finding out what they did during their free time, some girls told us that mainly they talked about other girls. Given the frequency of this activity, many girls were constantly confronted with the topic of female appearance.

It was evident from the girls' comments that the continual focus on other girls' looks further added to their anxieties about their own appearance.

> There was an interesting discussion between Peggy and Lisa about the girl that Bob is taking to the dance. They talked about whether she was cute or not and ended up agreeing that she was a stack of bones. That generated some discussion about weight and Lisa said that she [Lisa] was fat. Peggy said that she wasn't. Then Wendy wondered if she was a stack of bones and Lisa told her that no, she was just right—that she wasn't skinny and she wasn't fat either. [Stephanie's notes]

While these girls got reassurance from their friends that they were neither too fat nor too thin, in most cases girls did not openly reveal their concerns and thus did not receive such assurance. Instead, many girls were likely to remain self-conscious and insecure about their body type and weight.

Although gossip generated greater insecurity among these girls, it was extremely difficult to avoid participating in once it got started. In most gossip episodes, once someone supports the first critical remark, others join in and expand on this initial criticism.[6] As a result, girls may be drawn in and find themselves making negative evaluations of someone they don't even know. In the following example, the eighth-grade girls who previously referred to developed girls as "early figure people" were gossiping about a girl in choir who had particularly large breasts.[7]

> *Eighth Grade*
> PENNY: In choir that girl was sitting in front of us and we kept going "Moo."
> KAREN: We were going, "Come here cow. Come here cow."
> PENNY: And that girl kept going.
> BONNIE: I know. She is one.
> PENNY: She looks like a big|fat cow.
> JULIE: |Who is that?
> BONNIE: That girl on the basketball team |
> PENNY: |That big red-headed cow.|
> BONNIE: |From Clintonville.
> JULIE: Oh yeah. I know. She is a cow.

Penny began this episode by describing how they made fun of this girl in choir by saying "Moo." Karen was the first to expand on the gossip by adding more details to the story. Julie was apparently unfamiliar with the target initially, since she asked for further identification. Despite her initial confusion, however, she too joined the negative evaluation by the end, adding, "Oh yeah. I know. She is a cow."

This illustrates an important aspect of the highly collaborative nature of gossip. Since gossip mainly includes comments that support the initial evaluation, it is much easier to continue to develop the expressed viewpoint of a group than it is to challenge it.[8] Once someone makes a single supportive comment, no one challenges the collective evaluation. This means that someone who wanted to disagree with the negative evaluation of this girl would have to speak up immediately.

Changes in the Importance of Appearance Over Time

Because students at Woodview continually reinforced the importance of appearance for girls during their daily interactions, it was not surprising that girls in some of the groups began to spend more and more of their lunch period in the bathrooms trying to enhance their looks. Some days the focus was on experimenting with different types of makeup that one or more girls brought to school. Other days, girls would borrow curling irons and devote much of the period to changing their hairstyles.[9]

There was a definite change in certain girls' self-esteem and self-consciousness about their appearance. For example, one seventh-grade girl that I [Donna] sat with was very outgoing and confident at the beginning of the school year. A few months later she was starting to wear makeup and spend more time in the bathroom at lunch curling her hair. Although her general appearance and the fact that she was somewhat overweight had not seemed to bother her at all early in the year, she now seemed to be increasingly self-conscious about how she looked. There was also a dramatic change in her previously outgoing, confident manner as she became increasingly withdrawn. Other studies have found that around seventh grade, girls first report attaching more importance to appearance as well as being more critical of their own appearance than boys of the same age.[10]

While most of the peer activity seemed to reinforce the emphasis on good looks, there were a few noticeable exceptions. These occurred primarily among younger girls, who mocked the excessive concern they felt some women had with their appearance. For example, one day two sixth-graders were talking about a student teacher.

> They were talking about how thick her makeup is and how her face is really small but it gets really thick when she puts all this makeup on. Then Amy said, "Oh, I have to go now . . . my fiancé is coming in three hours and I have to fix my hair." [Donna's notes]

Even in seventh grade, some girls continued to mock the idea of enhancing one's beauty through artificial means like makeup. While most of the girls in Sally's group were showing increased concern with their own appearance, Sally was able to mock their obsession.

> Sally was looking in Linda's purse and putting on some makeup right at the lunch table. She put on some white eye shadow, which they all laughed at. Then she put on a lot of blue eye shadow and looked in the mirror, saying, "Oh, aren't I pretty?" It was interesting because she was making fun of something which many of the girls in this group are now starting to take more seriously. [Donna's notes]

This example shows that at least some girls in the school found ways to resist the growing concern with being more attractive. Unfortunately, by seventh grade there was little collective mocking of appearance. In a study of women at southern colleges, Dorothy Holland and Margaret Eisenhart also found that women had few opportunities to collectively resist the overriding preoccupation with attractiveness and romantic relationships.[11]

The Dilemma of Having No Control versus Exerting Too Much Control Over Appearance

Since gossip was the main vehicle for discussing appearance in this school, we will examine more closely the messages communicated through gossip. Naomi Wolf has noted that female gossip tends to promote the comparison of each other based on superficial standards.[12] In addition, girls are often compared regarding aspects of themselves over which they have little control.[13] For example, one typical form of gossip concerned the type of clothes worn by other girls. Girls from lower-working-class backgrounds often couldn't afford to buy name-brand clothes and shoes, and their attire was often subject to criticism by girls who could afford nicer clothes. Comments about people's clothes were often made loud enough for the targets to hear.

> As Lynn walked by they jeered at her and made fun of her. . . . One of these girls was going, "Oooh, look at those pants! Ohh, how could you wear those?" [Stephanie's notes]

At other times people were directly ridiculed.

> She also said that the cheerleaders made fun of people if they didn't wear Nike or Adidas shoes. They'd look at her and say, "Oh, where did you get your shoes?" She said that she just wears plain old tennis shoes. [Cathy's notes]

Besides being appraised on the basis of their attire, girls were also evaluated for their body weight and type. Girls who were particularly overweight were frequent targets of gossip, as in this extensive discussion of an isolate by several sixth-graders.

113

A large part of what these girls did today was make fun of one girl, Gloria. One girl would say, "Here is the airplane; the pilot says, 'Will somebody please come up front,' and all of a sudden somebody walks up front," showing with her hands how the plane dives. Then somebody else says, " Or here's the plane flying," and she shows it flying lopsided with her hands. "Then Gloria walks over to the other side and it flips the other way." Or, "Here's the airplane and there's a weak spot in the middle, and Gloria walks down the aisle and she falls through." [Stephanie's notes]

This episode continued with other jokes about Gloria, including using her as a trampoline in gym class and how she could serve as a windblock for all of them at once.

It was not just overweight girls who were made fun of and evaluated, however. Girls who were too skinny were also criticized, as were girls who had large hips or large breasts. Girls have no control over most of these physical characteristics. Perhaps because of the extensive nature of this type of gossip, girls often try to increase their control over their weight by dieting, which leads, in more severe cases, to eating disorders such as anorexia and bulimia. Although this focus on body weight may seem obsessive, it makes sense in light of the frequency of body critiques in girls' evaluative talk and in the media.

Given the importance of good looks for gaining status among peers and avoiding negative evaluations, it is not surprising that girls devote so much attention to their appearance. Ironically, another relatively frequent theme of gossip was negatively judging others for putting too much emphasis on their looks. Girls seemed particularly critical of girls who tried to stand out in some manner, either by dressing in a unique fashion or by making themselves "too attractive" or "too sexy."

As mentioned in chapter 4, girls did not perceive the status system within their school to be fair. Because of this and the fact that they were often judged on aspects of appearance beyond their control, many girls tended to feel unfairly rated. This could lead to feelings of frustration and jealousy, which may explain in part why girls were so critical of other girls who did stand out in some manner. This appeared to be one of the reasons why a group of sixth-graders spent much of one lunch period making fun of a popular girl for wearing a particularly unusual outfit to school.

> There was a long discussion throughout lunch about Jane, who I have been told before is the most popular girl in the sixth grade. Today she was wearing a khaki outfit, matching pants and a shirt—sort of a safari look. The first thing that got the conversation going was that Ilene started talking about a girl that had a "jungle suit" on. And Nicki, Jesse, and Kristy all sort of joined in with this conversation, and even Andrea played along with it for a while. They started out by saying that they'd seen her in the hall, given her the Tarzan yell, and she'd turned around and looked at them and they'd said, "Where'd you get the jungle outfit?" And they wondered if she was going to give the Tarzan yell back. They started talking about it as though she was Tarzan's monkey, Cheetah, and then the conversation sort of strayed from clothes and went to how she won the dog contest— how she's the number one dog of the school, which is the exact opposite since she's so popular. She does look older. She had her hair up, and had quite a bit of makeup on. [Stephanie's notes]

In another case, a group of eighth-grade girls was critical of a local beauty pageant contestant of high school age who visited the school to collect money for her campaign. In this case, they claimed that she used makeup to give a false image of beauty, and that underneath she was really ugly.[14]

115

Eighth Grade

PENNY: I'm not giving it to her.

CINDY: The only thing that makes her look anything is all the makeup|and [unclear]

PENNY: |She had a picture and she's standing there like this, she's going [Poses with one hand on her hip and one by her head]

CINDY: Her face is probably this skinny but it looks that big cuz of all the makeup|she has on it.

PENNY: |She's *ugly*, ugly, ugly! [In a low voice]

BONNIE: She looks like a cow.

This girl was criticized for her attempts to be "too attractive" and "too sexy." In her case, a flirtatious pose in one of her photographs was seen as evidence of trying to be too sexy. More often girls complained about the attire of their peers, saying their clothes were too skimpy or revealing. For example, a girl who wore a loose-fitting top to the school picnic was the target of two seventh-graders' gossip.

BARBIE: I'm getting sick.

ANNIE: And she lets her tits hang.

BARBIE: She does. They hang out the side and she acts like she doesn't know.

ANNIE: Yeah.

BARBIE: Let's go look|on

ANNIE: |And she goes and plays volleyball and they pop out the top and she knows|it.

BARBIE: |And the sides.

STEPHANIE: Are you kidding?

ANNIE: And she knows, too.

This particular girl was being doubly criticized. Not only did she wear an outfit that they considered too revealing, but she acted as if she was unaware of just how revealing this outfit was. Since these girls believed that she was fully aware that her top exposed her breasts, they found her denial to be an even greater offense.

Some of the strongest gossip was aimed at girls who stood out because of their weight and then drew further attention to themselves by wearing overly revealing attire.[15] This was evident when an obese girl wore very tight shorts to school one day. Natalie drew the group's attention to Amanda by conveying her disgust in a loud, rather shrill voice.

NATALIE: Oh my God!! Amanda Perkins is in shorts!! [unclear] me out! *Yucch!* [Shrill voice] and they're *tight as hell* on her!
[?]:   Where?
NATALIE: [In a shrill voice] Over *there* by the catsup stand!!
PEG: Jesus Christ!
NATALIE: Oh my God.
PEG: Ugh—that's gross! That is *real* gross. You don't *have* to look for it.
BILL: I wouldn't want to.
PEG: She *stands* out like a sore thumb.

The strong reaction against standing out conveyed in this episode and the ones that precede it show that gossip is a powerful form of social management. By criticizing other girls who stand out in some way, girls are reinforcing the importance of looking like everyone else. In her study of high school girls, Sue Lees also found that unique appearance and attempts to stand out are regarded very negatively.[16] Girls expect each other to be attractive, but only in a socially conforming way. This further takes girls' appearance out of their control by limiting the individuality of their self-presentations.

These different themes of gossip add to the already confusing message girls receive about their appearance. On the one hand they are continually faced with media messages that emphasize the importance of using makeup and fashionable attire to enhance their attractiveness and their sexuality. If they do succeed in looking, acting, or dressing like the models they see in the media, however, they are likely to be accused of portraying false images or wanton sexuality. Furthermore, this practice of criticizing the objects of sexual gaze deflects criticism away from boys and men for viewing girls in this limited manner. Thus, girls blame each other for drawing sexual attention to themselves rather than criticizing the social practices that promote a view of girls and women as sexual objects.

Insults About Appearance

Concerns about attractiveness were also communicated through insults, which, as we have seen before, tend to be an especially powerful means of reinforcing these concerns. The most common insult that boys aimed at girls was "dog." Some of the girls were skilled at ritual insulting and had quick comebacks, as in the following exchange.

> *Eighth Grade*
> BOY: All you girls are dogs.
> ELLEN: Ah, but you're a real fox.

Even though some girls were able to end such insult exchanges quickly, frequent appearance insults by boys further reinforce the message that boys have the power to rank girls by this superficial criterion.

By far most of the appearance insults were aimed at the few girls in the school who were social isolates. Some isolates were considered unattractive and were avoided because no one wanted to be associated with a girl that others considered unattractive.[17] This strongly demonstrates how significant appearance concerns were in this school. In addition, the very process of insulting isolates about their appearance further reinforced the importance of looks. Through such insults, being unattractive and having low status became increasingly associated with each other. Thus, in the end, the practice of insulting isolates increased all girls' anxiety about their appearance.

Some of the isolates developed self-defense skills and were able to keep the insulting at a less hostile level by responding with counterinsults. This was true of Helen, who was still an isolate in her eighth-grade year.

Eighth Grade

DANA: You act like you're hot stuff. You're ugly, Helen.
HELEN: You *are* ugly, aren't ya?
DANA: Just cool your ass down a little before I |
HELEN: |Cool
your ass off, Dana. Put it in some cool water; maybe it'll cool.
DANA: Aw, shut up.
HELEN: Why don't you make me?
DANA: I don't|
HELEN: |Kiss my grits!

In other cases, the nature of the insulting made it difficult for girls to have an effective response. For example, one day a group of eighth-grade girls were insulting Sally, a special education student. First they got up when she sat down next to them, saying, "Ooooh!" Then they kept telling each other to say, "Hey Sally!" and then bark.[18] Rather than call Sally a dog or accuse her of being ugly directly, their insults took a more indirect form, which would be difficult for anyone to respond to playfully. In cases like this, the person targeted by the insults was less able to respond in a ritual manner and often ended up feeling embarrassed and/or humiliated.

Another typical way of insulting an isolate was for a boy to pretend that he or a friend was sexually attracted to her. The implication is that because a girl is unpopular and/or unattractive, it is hilarious to tell her she is attractive.

> Frank said that Hal made fun of Belinda by telling her that she was good-looking and foxy. Hal denied that he was making fun of her and said that he thought she was [good-looking] and really fun . . . I've heard many people make fun of her and say things like this. [Steve's notes]

This type of ridicule, which consists of "reverse insults," is very difficult to respond to since it does not make sense to respond with a counterinsult. This leaves isolates few effective strategies for dealing with such offenses. At the same time, it strongly reinforces the norm that girls must be attractive to be of interest to boys.

Attractiveness as an Increasing Concern for Girls

Appearance is already a salient concern among these students, and it is likely to increase in importance for many as they get older. The number of school-sponsored contests that emphasize attractiveness increases in high school as girls are selected for pompom teams, cheerleading, baton twirlers in marching bands, and so on. In most of these cases, girls choose to enter these contests, although sometimes this "choice" may be the result of maternal pressure. A more powerful form of school-sponsored competition is the selection of prom queens, homecoming queens, and attendants in which girls are annually evaluated on their attractiveness, often without ever volunteering to enter such competitions. Generally, school officials assume that every girl in the school wants to enter, which implies that all girls wish to be judged on the basis of their appearance. At the same time, diverse subcultures often develop within large high schools, some of which place less emphasis on stereotypical gender concerns such as appearance.[19]

All of these contests send girls a strong message that what they do and who they are is less important than how they look. Even girls in achievement roles, such as basketball team members, continue to receive messages about the importance of appearance.[20] Such an emphasis prepares girls for adult careers and occupations where appearance continues to be an explicit or implicit basis for hiring and retaining employees.[21]

Unfortunately, this preoccupation with appearance seems to be increasing rather than decreasing over time. Many have argued that despite the women's movement, appearance pressures on women are unrelenting.[22] Some even argue that the escalating emphasis on appearance is part of the backlash against the women's movement.[23] Others have argued that, with the increase in cosmetic surgery, the boundaries of what is considered attractive or even "normal" continue to shrink.[24] For example, small or sagging breasts are now considered medically treatable problems, along with excess weight in buttocks, thighs, and stomachs.

Joyce Ladner's research on black adolescent girls indicates that they share this strong preoccupation with beauty and with makeup, hairstyles, and fashionable clothing.[25] Patricia Hill Collins, however, has expressed concern that the definition of what is attractive in this society reflects a white, middle-class bias. As

Collins notes, the unfortunate aspect of attractiveness comparisons is that someone needs to be considered ugly for another person to be viewed as beautiful. All too often these "someones" are women of color as well as working-class women.[26]

It is clear that appearance evaluations often influence women's sense of self-worth. Kathy Davis found that some women have so deeply internalized a negative view of their own bodies that they turn to cosmetic surgery to end a form of suffering that they consider "too strong to endure." Although the suffering was real to these women, Davis herself was generally unable to determine what body problem they sought to correct surgically until they told her.[27]

The fact that appearance concerns were communicated most frequently through gossip among peers at Woodview makes them particularly hard to address. As shown previously and again in the "cow" episode, gossip needed to be challenged immediately if opposition was to be expressed. While girls did challenge perceptions of other girls being snobs and flirts, they seldom challenged claims that other girls were ugly or inappropriately dressed. Instead, girls as well as boys often joined in negative evaluations of girls' appearance simply to be part of the conversation.[28]

Although appearance concerns were found at all status and class levels in this school, the nature of the concerns varied somewhat by social class. Girls from middle-class backgrounds spent much more time fixing their hair and trying to imitate the hairstyles of cheerleaders and other esteemed girls and women. They also made more comments than working-class girls about wearing the right name-brand clothes, wearing pants of the right length, and other details about conformity in dress. Girls from working-class backgrounds were not as concerned about the neatness of their hair or whether their shirts were tucked in properly, but they would comment on clothing that looked unusual to them because it was out-of-date or involved unusual combinations. They were also somewhat more likely to make general assessments of other girls' ugliness than were the middle-class girls. Concerns about excessive makeup and revealing clothing were found at all class and status levels, so it was not the case that working-class girls had different standards in this regard from those of middle-class girls.

Unfortunately, girls at all social class levels further create an arena for viewing girls as objects. Since girls and women are so used to being judged by superficial criteria and noticed primarily for their appearance, a related form of objectifying girls is likely also to seem normal—sexual objectification. It is to the entire area of developing views regarding romance and sexuality that we turn next.

8

"We May Be Friends with Them, But We're Not Sluts"

During the course of a given school day girls are likely to be confronted by many messages regarding their sexuality. We have already seen how the predominant message received by boys is that sexuality is another arena for competition. With girls, the messages are more complex, and sometimes contradictory. While media images of adolescent girls often depict them as being sexually sophisticated, parents and other adults in their lives suggest that they should be sexually naive. Perhaps due to media influence, girls and their peers tend to be impressed with a certain degree of sexual knowledge and sophistication. However, both boys and girls are likely to send strong messages that being *too* sexual, or even having an active sense of sexuality, is inappropriate. All these confusing messages are conveyed within a context where heterosexuality is the only acceptable sexual preference, so it is this topic that we turn to first.

The Construction of Heterosexuality

Girls conveyed their belief that only heterosexual feelings were appropriate in many ways. Labels such as "queer" and "gay" were generally given negative connotations, even though the meaning of these terms was often a source of confusion.[1] For example, one day an eighth-grade girl was discussing her sixth-grade sister, whom she considered a tomboy.

> Kerry said her sister is extremely different from her and has absolutely no interest in boys; she considers them pests. She referred to her sister as a tomboy. She said since she is a tomboy, if she liked boys then she would be queer, but on the other hand, if she liked girls then she would *really* be queer. Then Ellie added jokingly that if she didn't like anyone at all she would still be queer. I said, "It sounds like she doesn't have a chance." [Cathy's notes]

This labeling of Kerry's sister illustrates the confusion many adolescents experience regarding sexual identity and preference. A girl who likes other girls would be considered queer, but what about a more "boyish" girl who likes boys? Would she be queer as well? And what about a girl who likes male activities and has no particular sexual attraction to anyone? Does that make her queer, too? Labeling girls "queer" who express nontraditional interests makes it very difficult for them to experiment with and pursue a variety of different interests in adolescence.

The negative view of homosexuality that was being developed was further intensified by the fact that social isolates were most frequently labeled homosexual. As shown in chapter 4, people who were negatively evaluated for one reason, whether their perceived unattractive appearance or their lower intellectual

126

achievement, were often the targets of sexual evaluations as well. While boys would tend to ridicule these people openly, girls were more likely to gossip about them.

> Annie said, "I'm going to beat that girl up someday," re-
> ferring to an overweight girl with a green sweater on who
> was sitting at the middle table next to the twins. We all
> turned to look at her, and Marsha agreed that she was
> really disgusting and that "she's gay." [Stephanie's notes]

There was no discussion about why this girl was perceived to be gay. It was simply another negative evaluation attached to a girl who was overweight and therefore "disgusting." Through their gossip, girls express their social distance from such girls as well as reinforcing the strong norm of heterosexuality.

Since girls at this age have intimate friendships, some of which include a high degree of physical contact, teasing was an important means for clarifying that expressions of affection should not be regarded as homosexual.[2] For example one day, a small girl came over and sat on Andrea's lap. Andrea responded by laughing and saying, "You're really not my type." In another instance, two girls were described as being "best mates." Immediately Mia said, "Oooooh . . . ," implying that this might mean they were gay. Hillary picked up on that and said, "Ooooh" as well. In both cases, the message being conveyed was that while intimacy between girls is okay, homosexuality is not. Girls themselves make similar attempts to distinguish their affectionate feelings from homosexual ones. For example, one day Sally told her friends that she always signs her letters, "Love you dearly, but not queerly."

Within Woodview, we saw only one example of people mocking this overriding concern with heterosexuality. One day a group of eighth-grade girls spent part of their lunch period singing a song they had made up. In this song they substituted the phrase "We're queer forever" for the standard refrain, "We're friends forever." Other adolescent girls have also used music to challenge the heterosexual norm. For example, when I [Donna] was walking in our neighborhood park one day I overheard the following song being sung by two adolescent girls as they walked together arm in arm.

> I love you. You love me.
> Homosexuality.
> Some people think we're just friends.
> But we're really lesbians.

This suggests that in some communities, adolescent females are choosing to directly challenge the norm of heterosexuality.[3] However, at Woodview heterosexuality is reinforced as the only valid option of sexual orientation. Michelle Fine's research shows this to be true for other public schools as well.[4]

The Negative Labeling of Female Sexuality

Since heterosexuality was by far the predominant frame in this school environment, it is critical that we better understand the nature of heterosexual images within the context of gender inequality. So far in this book we have shown how boys tend to perceive girls as objects for sexual conquest as they compete with other boys for sexual achievements. In chapter 7, we showed how girls are increasingly influenced at this age to base their self-worth on their physical attractiveness. This focus further creates an image of girls as being passive and the objects of others' gaze. Within this context it is not surprising that girls are judged primarily by their desirability as attractive sexual partners.

One day a group of seventh-grade boys had a conversation about the girls they liked. The primary focus of the conversation was the girls' appearance and sexual allure. This led to a series of ritual insults about each other's girlfriends.

> Hank pointed toward the parking lot and said, "There's Kim. She's nasty." Eric said that she wasn't and that he thought she looked good. Hank said no; she piles all that makeup on and looks like a whore. He kept repeating "a whore" while Eric tried to tell me and/or Hank that she wasn't. During all this time Joe was going from our group back to the group of girls. Now he came up and lay down on top of the wall. He said, "Ah, it's just lust, just lust." Eric said that's why Joe was after Tammy. Joe said he was right and Hank said, "She's got a great body, but a nasty face. She's a fox all right, a member of the dog family." [Steve's notes]

Because girlfriends are often seen as the property of the boys they are going with, male competition includes judgments or evaluations of each others' girlfriends. These boys, who dated the highest status girls in the school, still accentuated perceived physical flaws in each other's girlfriends. While these boys were interested in girls with "great bodies," some were critical of girls who drew too much attention to their sexuality through use of makeup, labeling them "whores." This conveys the clear message that girls should be passive sexual objects, that it is important that they not draw *too* much attention to their sexuality.

While girls could be labeled whores and sluts simply on the basis of their "overly sexual" appearance, girls who demonstrated an even more active stance toward sexuality had a greater chance of being negatively labeled. What was considered acceptable behavior in boys—making sexual passes at other boy's girlfriends as well as at their own girlfriends—was definitely not considered acceptable in girls. Those girls who did initiate sexual actions were labeled "bitches" and "sluts."

> After Mike was out of earshot they started saying what a bitch Kim was. I asked why this was so. Hank replied that she uses guys; she always went with real worms and then messed around with everyone else. Hank said that when she went with Bradley she was always playing with his ass, saying, "Oh, it's just so cute, I can't resist."
> [Steve's notes]

Kim was criticized for being indiscriminate in her advances. Furthermore, Hank was critical of Kim's sexual assertiveness with her own boyfriend. Clearly, she was being negatively labeled because she violated these boys' view that girls should be objects for their own sexual advances but not actors in their own right.

In these cases, girls were evaluated behind their backs. Boys, however, were just as likely to insult girls directly for being too sexual. Labels such as "slut" and "whore" were the most commonly used and might be aimed at any girl in the lunchroom. For example, one day Joe and Hank walked over to a girl sitting at a table and repeatedly called her "slut-face" and "whore". They asked if her rates had gone down, or if they were still a quarter. They also told her they knew she'd "fuck any guy in the school." Her only comeback was to say they couldn't find Hank's IQ. Hank responded by saying, "Oh, that's really gay." Then he repeated what she had said and laughed. She finally said, "Fuck you," at which point Hank and Joe backed off and left her alone.

This episode is typical of insult exchanges among boys. If the target of the insult does not offer a good challenge early on, the exchange tends to escalate to a more serious level. Because girls are less likely to engage in ritual insulting than boys, they are often less prepared to defend themselves in such exchanges. As a result, they become easy targets for sexual harassment. Furthermore, insults such as "slut" and "whore" imply that boys do not believe that girls should be sexually active or have a variety of boyfriends, while such behaviors are viewed as normal and acceptable for boys.

Perhaps more surprising is the extent to which girls themselves use similar insults to limit each others' sexuality. At first, pejorative labels such as "slut" and "bitch" were aimed primarily at girls they believed to be purposely stealing their boyfriends. For example, during seventh grade a group of girls explained that while several girls might end up liking the same boy, this was different from having someone try to take a boy "away from you." A number of girls at this age also admitted to having "gone with" several boys at once, even though this was against their developing view that girls should only like one boy at a time.[5]

By eighth grade, these same girls had started to monitor each other's sexual thoughts and behaviors to a much greater degree. Most of the girls now had a single boyfriend and would critically refer to those friends who failed to show any discretion in their sexual interests as sluts. Sometimes the insults aimed at these girls were responded to jokingly, as in the following example.

Eighth Grade
TRICIA: Ellen, you've got a dirty mind.
ELLEN: I'm not dirty [less audible] [Squealing, then she breaks down in laughs and coughs before she can complete sentence.]
NATALIE: Look at look at Ellen. [To boys] Give you somethin' to think about, what's goin' on in this world.
PEG: Yeah, the gutter.
BOY: No
[To suggestion he look at Ellen]

NATALIE: The gutter [Giggles] That was a good one.
BOYS: Who is it?
ELLEN: It's better than what *you* were, which is a piece
of |shit.
TRICIA: |Shit.

Even though Ellen responded playfully to these insults by laughing and insulting back, an important message is conveyed about
the inappropriateness of having a "dirty mind." There are several
possible reasons why these girls rely on insults that are so restric-
tive of their sexuality. Jealousies are likely to play some role
since they were often evident in cases of female sexual insulting
While boys develop other strategies to deal with sexual competition,, such as aggressively defending their sexual "property," girls
may rely more on insulting to control others' unwanted sexual
initiations. This possibility is supported by the fact that this type
of insulting increased between seventh grade and eighth grade as
girls experienced more hurt feelings over losing boyfriends to
other girls. Also, as girls become more aware of the negative
connotations associated with female active sexuality, they may
wish to avoid association with girls whose behavior could be
considered promiscuous. However, by using insults such as these
to control certain unwanted sexual behaviors, girls end up reinforcing the strong constraints that society places on their own
sexuality and that of all women.

Another obvious reason for girls' sexual insulting is the lack of
an alternative discourse. As both Sue Lees and Valerie Walkerdine
have noted, there is no such thing as a "natural language," and the
discourse of adolescent subcultures will continue to reproduce
oppressive realities until alternative discourses are available.[6] In
their studies of older adolescent girls in Britain, Sue Lees and
Helena Wulff report that sexual labels such as "slut," "slag," and
"whore" are commonly used by both girls and boys. These labels
are applied to girls who are sexually active with more than one

boy, even though such behavior is viewed as normative for boys. They are also applied to girls who have a number of boyfriends or who are seen talking with a number of boys, as well as to more independent girls who aren't attached to a boy or who go places on their own.[7] The only solution the girls in Lees's study found for avoiding this label or redeeming a negative reputation was to get a steady boyfriend. As she notes, "language defines our possibilities and limitations." Labels like "slut" and "whore" place a double standard of morality directly into our language and thus into our consciousness. Active sexuality becomes perceived as "normal" for males and "abnormal" for females. Consequently, rather than challenge the labels themselves, girls seek to avoid being called these names by getting long-term boyfriends and, eventually, by getting married.[8]

Attempts by Individual Girls to Resist Sexual Labels

The rules of insult exchanges offer girls few opportunities for challenging such insults. As mentioned earlier in this book, the expected response to an insult is a counterinsult. There is, thus, little chance ever to confront the content of the insults themselves. Girls never challenge the negative implication of these insults with comments such as "So what?" or "Who cares?" Furthermore, to get angry at the use of an insult based on an unfair norm was viewed as not following the rules of the game, since people are expected to be able to handle being insulted by others. This is evident in the following example, when Ellen gets angry at being referred to as a slut. This exchange begins as Tricia responds to a question asked by me [Cathy] concerning the importance of boys in her life. Natalie expands on her answer by distinguishing her views from those of some of her friends, using the term "slut" to refer to their total focus on boys and sex.

Eighth Grade Interview with Cathy

TRICIA: I feel the same way that Peg does, especially now when we're just about to go into high school our grades are more important than boys.

NATALIE: See, we may be friends with them, but we're not sluts.

HANNAH: Will you repeat that please? [Angry tone]

TRICIA: No, you don't qualify.

NATALIE: I know, but we're not sluts.

ELLEN: [Unclear] fuck you you guys! [Ellen stomps off angrily.]

NATALIE: Well *look* at that! She does that every time!

HANNAH: She's pissed at *me*. She's pissed at me because I want to fight her and she doesn't—and she won't fight me.

ELLEN: [Calls from another part of the room.] What did *you* do the last time you remember that [less audible] Natalie?

NATALIE: I stayed *around* ta fight ya! [Laughs]

CATHY: Are her feelings really hurt or is she just pretending?

HANNAH: [Unclear] around when *I* wanted to fight. I told her to call me when she wants to fight.

NATALIE: She—*every* time, every time I—we call her a name she takes it *seriously* and *goes* off and *pouts*.

PEG: She calls *us* names all the time.

NATALIE: And she calls *us* names *every* day.

TRICIA: She'll *call* ya a *bitch* for no reason. [In a low voice]

This example shows how difficult it is for girls to challenge sexual insults. While boys are expected to be continually interested in sex, girls are expected to limit their interest. Since this social message is conveyed mainly through insults such as "slut," it is very difficult for girls to challenge the implied expectation that boys can be more sexually active than girls. In fact, a person who expresses anger at the insult is viewed as not playing according to the rules of verbal dueling. Here, the mode of talk along with the social message puts girls in a double constraint, one from which even the cleverest girls have trouble breaking away.

The two cases in which a girl was able to resist negative sexual labeling successfully both involved the same sixth-grader, Andrea. One day she was collecting money for a candy sale and had five or six dollars in an envelope. Walter, a former boyfriend and current friend, made a few comments about her collecting money as a prostitute. She responded to him by saying that she "wasn't that low and wasn't that cheap." Then she challenged Walter, saying now that he brought it up she remembered that he owed her some money. Walter replied saying, "I don't owe you anything. You enjoyed it, didn't you?" He then gave her a nickel, and Andrea said, "Well, I'm not that cheap."

Because Andrea had good bantering skills she was able to keep the insulting at a playful level. In fact, the degree of rapport between Andrea and Walter, as well as their strong verbal skills, led to an unusually playful insult exhange. In the process, some stereotypical notions about female sexuality were challenged when Walter claimed that because Andrea enjoyed it he didn't owe her anything.[9]

In the other case, Andrea was complaining to her friends that a popular girl was being labeled a slut unfairly. She then said that if anybody called her a slut or a whore they wouldn't be around long to say it again. After that she related a story about a guy down the street from her who called her a bitch. She had responded by punching him in the stomach and said he claimed he threw up on the way home because she had punched him so hard.

Here Andrea's physical size and strength are important assets. The fact that she is larger and stronger than many boys her age gives her a definite advantage. Also, it is possible that an angry response is more acceptable when one is insulted by an acquaintance rather than by a group member. Whereas friends may expect you to treat insults nonseriously, insulting between acquaintances is more likely to escalate into anger and/or physical fighting.

While both of these strategies worked well for Andrea, it is not surprising that they were not more commonly found. First, few girls in this school had the level of ritual insulting skills that Andrea possessed. Also, while many of the girls were still physically larger than boys their age, only a few girls reported engaging in physical fights with boys. Furthermore, those girls who did have reputations for fighting were seldom insulted by boys. Nevertheless, Andrea's example does show the value of developing verbal strategies for responding to sexual insults.

In her study of older girls, Sue Lees found that the most common response to sexual insulting was to deny the label, but not to challenge the implied double standard.[10] Other responses included trying to ignore comments or boys altogether, resigning themselves to gross behavior without feeling threatened by it, and actively challenging boys by calling them names. Although this last strategy is the most assertive, it was only moderately successful, because there are fewer negative cultural associations with male promiscuity, and girls who did talk back to boys were often labeled sluts because of this assertive behavior. However, some of the girls in the Lees study were beginning to question these labels and become aware of their sexist nature and implied double standard.

Avoiding Sexual Innocence

The negative labeling of female sexuality is further compounded by girls' desire to avoid seeming sexually innocent or prudish. For some girls, part of entering adolescence is a rejection of childhood. For many of these girls, this includes a rejection of sexual innocence. By presenting a different view of themselves—one in which they appear as sexually knowledgeable—these girls are actively challenging adult notions of adolescent girls' sexuality.

Most of this presentation of themselves as sexually knowledgeable occurred through the process of storytelling. As we have seen, storytelling is a very flexible activity, allowing for the simultaneous expression of multiple viewpoints. This makes it an ideal mode in which to contrast adult conceptions of adolescent girls' sexuality with those of their peers. For example, one day several eighth-grade girls collectively told a story about an incident during study hall in which some boys tried to get a book away from one of them. They then went on to mock the teacher's reaction upon seeing the book—"I hope you know that's a dirty book." What these girls found humorous was the teacher's view of them as sexually naive in that she expected them to be neither aware of the sexual content of the book nor interested in reading about it.

In another storytelling episode, two sixth-graders jointly described a comedy routine they saw with their parents. Of particular interest to them were some of the more sexually explicit aspects of the skits and their parents' reaction to the girls having witnessed these scenes. For example, one skit centered around the theme of defective condoms.

Sixth Grade
ANDREA: He reached down his pants and he pulled out a balloon.
MARLA: Oooooh! [Laughs]
ANDREA: And he goes—Marla shut up! and uh he goes "Shit you gotta test these things that woulda been a that woulda been two babies!"
MARLA: He's dirty!

ANDREA: I couldn't get over that. Oh it was funny. [Sentence less audible].

MARLA: My mamma was sittin' there goin', "Oh my God!" [Laughs]

ANDREA: My dad I'll bet you he goes, "Oh my God, my little girl's here." [Laughs] I would've said listen, I wo—wo—would've said, "Listen honey, I know all about it already."

STEPHANIE: I was gonna say he looks up and sees you laughing and goes [Has a puzzled expression on her face] [Laughs]

After Andrea describes one of the scenes, Marla adds her mother's concerned reaction, which she finds amusing. Andrea immediately picks up on this and offers an imaginary account of her father's reaction, which emphasizes his view of her as a "little," and thus naive, girl. In contrast, her response turns the tables, making him appear to be the naive parent and her the sophisticated adolescent.

Other real and imaginary narratives were enhanced by girls displaying their worldly awareness and knowledge. Sexual content made these narratives more entertaining, enhancing the quality of the girls' performances and their ability to hold the attention and interest of others. For example, one day Laura and Jack were making jokes about the name of Jack's new nephew, Gideon. They developed a collaborative performance that began with other themes and then became more sexual, with comments such as "Gideon the bed" ("Giddy on the bed") and "Gideon in and Gideon out." Some of the girls sitting around the table were hesitant to react at first but soon found themselves laughing along with everyone else.

Through their narratives and performances girls attempted to avoid seeming to be sexually innocent. Boys face a similar issue of wanting to appear sexually sophisticated. Un-

like boys, girls who have too much sexual interest or assertiveness are also to be scorned. And, as many girls know, the thin
line between being sexual enough without being too sexual is
often a continually disappearing one. Because girls fear being
ostracized for sexual activity as well as sexual innocence, Michelle Fine found that few girls were willing to speak up in sex
education discussions.[11] Also, as Sue Lees points out, whether
girls are labeled for being too sexually available or too "tight,"
they are being defined in relation to men whether they want
to be or not.[12]

Challenging Romantic and Sexual Messages Through Collaborative Teasing

Collaborative teasing was even more popular than storytelling as
a means of challenging stereotypical views of feminine behavior.
Because teasing is based on mockery, it is an ideal form of speech
for challenging and making fun of beliefs regarding feminine
behavior. Some of the romantic and sexual teasing consisted simply of claims that friends were "in love" with particular boys.
However, most of this teasing also included mocking stereotypes
of romance and sexuality. For example, some girls made fun of
traditional ways in which women manipulate men through plead-
ing and crying, as well as getting male attention through flirtatious talk and behavior. In other cases, girls mocked gender roles
through the use of role reversal, such as exerting physical dominance over boys by playfully pushing them to the floor.

In the following example, a group of eighth-grade girls
flirted to gain male attention while simultaneously mocking the
stereotype of women engaging in this behavior. This group of

five girls and one boy was sitting around a table in the media center during lunch period. When Ted, a fellow classmate, walked by, Ellen tried to get his attention, calling, "Oh Ted," with a slight lilt in her voice. Her friend, Natalie, picked up on this and exaggerated the underlying flirtatious tone. (Natalie had previously gone with Jimmy for two days. When Jimmy broke up with her he told her that he liked her and wanted to go with her again but that he had "some things he had to straighten out first." She still liked Jimmy, but he was now more interested in Rhoda, another group member, which made Natalie prone to jealousy when Jimmy was around.)

Eighth Grade

ELLEN: Oh Ted! When do we have to have our pictures turned in?

NATALIE: Oh Ted! [Speaks in high, mocking, flirtatious tone, then giggles]

PAM: Oh Ted! [Same tone]

ELLEN: Oh Ted! [Same tone]

RHODA: Ted. [Same tone]

[?]: Ted. [Same tone]

JIMMY: Ted. [Same tone, putting a hand lightly on Ellen's shoulder]

ELLEN: Ohh Jimmy. [Same tone, touching Jimmy's arm]

NATALIE: [To Ellen, leaning across table and tapping her on arm] You're not supposed to go, "Oh Jimmy;" you're supposed to go, "Ohhh, Jim!" [Gives words a blatantly sexual emphasis; leans back, claps hands together, and laughs giddily] [General laughter]

JIMMY: Oh man.

ELLEN [?]: That is

JIMMY: ridiculous. [Poking Ellen under table]

ELLEN: Eek! [Slaps Jimmy on the arm]

NATALIE: Sorry. [Still giggling]

After Natalie initiated the teasing, all of the other group members joined in by imitating this high, flirtatious tone of voice. Ellen even mocked herself when she turned to Jimmy and said, "Ohh Jimmy," with the same coy intonation. Not only did the very nature of teasing allow these girls an opportunity to mock stereotypical feminine behavior, it allowed Ellen the opportunity to easily mimic herself by tying it to the mockery of a feminine role.

Up to this point, the entire group seemed to be enjoying this entertaining activity. However, when Ellen directed her flirtatious tone at Jimmy, it apparently triggered Natalie's jealousy, as she then attempted to stop the teasing by escalating it. This was done by changing the tone of her voice from flirtation to sexual desire. The result was a moment of intense embarrassment on the part of all group members. But the playful tone was quickly restored when Jimmy teasingly poked Ellen as he and Ellen jointly commented on the inappropriateness of Natalie's comment.

Shortly after this episode, Pam and Ellen began affectionately teasing Jimmy with more verbal and physical attention. Pam told Jimmy his hair was messed up and needed to be combed as she reached over and mussed his hair. When Jimmy pretended to leave, Ellen and Pam started a mock battle over him, pulling on him from both sides and ordering him to stay. Natalie again tried to end the teasing episode by making a serious command.

PAM   [To Jimmy] Your hair's messed up. Gotta comb it. [Tricia messes up Jimmy's hair with hand. Jimmy moves as if to leave.]

ELLEN: Stay here, Jim. [Jimmy and Pam begin to wrestle.]

PAM: No! Stay here. [Laughing; both Pam and Ellen are pulling on Jimmy.]

NATALIE: [To Ellen and Pam] Leave his hair alone. It's not your property. It's not mine either.

JIMMY: [To Pam] I've been insulted. I gotta go. I've been insulted. [Jimmy is smiling, looking at Pam, and is waving his arms around as though trying to keep the girls away.]

141

ELLEN: [Grins at Natalie and then reaches under table and tickles Jimmy on thigh.] It's mine! [Laughing]

JIMMY: Oh ho-ho.

NATALIE: I said it wasn't mine.

ELLEN: It's my property. [Reaching out and touching Jimmy]

PAM: It's mine. [Ellen pulls Jimmy's chair a little toward her and then puts hand on Jimmy's shoulder and pushes him to floor.]

JIMMY: [To Pam] She made me sit on the floor. [Jimmy gets up off floor and walks away.]

ELLEN: Jim, if you don't get up here [Pointing to chair he was sitting in] I'll have someone kiss you [unclear]

NATALIE: I will. [Whispering.]

RHODA: [To Jimmy] Natalie will!

Throughout this episode we can see how these girls used teasing to mock stereotypical feminine behaviors and engage in alternative ones. They continually pushed Jimmy around and ordered him to stay put. Through satire, they transformed the concept of ownership to one in which boys are the property of girls instead of vice versa. Finally, by pretending to fight physically over Jimmy, Pam and Ellen mocked the stereotypical notion that girls are always competing for boys. This is especially interesting because there was real competition for Jimmy's attention among other girls in this group. Perhaps Natalie's friends were trying to pull her back to her more typical lighthearted attitude. However, Natalie appeared to be starting to take boyfriends more seriously and seemed unable at this point to detach from her competitive and jealous feelings.

Shortly after this episode, Ellen initiated yet another teasing episode. Jimmy had still not returned to the group, so Ellen first commanded him to return and then threatened to start crying.

After a complaint by Rhoda, Natalie joined in by pretending to whine as a way of getting Jimmy to comply. Finally, Ellen joined in by ordering him and then giving him a sexual threat.

ELLEN: [To Jimmy] Get over here! [Puts fist on table for emphasis] I'll start to cryin'.
RHODA: [Softly and urgently] Ellen, would ya shut up, you're getting us in trouble. Just [unclear] because of you.
NATALIE: [To Jimmy] Come o'er here and sit down Ple-e-ease. [Whining tone] [At this point all of the girls are looking in Jimmy's direction.]
RHODA [?]:   Jim.
ELLEN: [Tapping loudly on table with a pencil] Jim, c'mere or I'll do some thing.
[?]:   Nothing
NATALIE: [In a higher intonation] Please sit down.
[Jimmy walks back over.]
ELLEN: I'll ruin your family life. [Jimmy sits down.]
JIMMY: Oh! [Laughs, with others]

All of these comments convey detachment from stereotypical roles, either mocking behavior such as crying and whining to get one's way or reversing roles, with girls being sexually aggressive. Working-class girls such as these girls have often been portrayed as being primarily concerned with romance and femininity.[13] These episodes suggest that rather than embracing traditional notions of romance, many girls feel free to use them as a resource for creating their own gender dynamics.

While girls included sexual themes as part of their playful talk, it was not as frequent as romantic teasing. When it did occur, it sometimes led to intense embarrassment. The following sexual/romantic teasing episode took place among a group of seventh-grade girls who were seated in the lunchroom on the day of the class picnic. Ginny began the teasing by developing an imaginary scenario in which a tape recorder is present when Annie and her boyfriend are together having sex, or at least trying to have sex.

Seventh Grade

GINNY: You know what you guys are gonna say "Oh Bob" "Annie" [unclear] tape record you're gonna listen to it [less audible] and say "Oh Bob it feels so good." [Laughter]

ANNIE: You ain't gonna hear that cause I ain't doin' nothin'.

BARBIE: "[Unclear] deeper!" [Laughter]

GINNY: "Little bit higher Barbie [unclear] little bit higher [unclear] little bit higher."

ANNIE: [Loud groan]

BARBIE: "What can I do?! Are we doin' it yet?! Uh spread your legs a little more and [unclear]."

MARSHA: [Makes a kind of sign to Barbie] *Forever!* [A popular novel written for adolescents]

BARBIE: In and out *Forever!*

GINNY: Insert outsert. She goes—Annie. [Sentence less audible]

[?]:   In out in out.

ANNIE: [Unclear] If she seems to be cryin' it's a moment of joy! [Laughter]

Ginny begins this teasing episode by making an explicit reference to Annie's sexual enjoyment, acting out her role by saying, "Oh Bob, it feels so good." This apparently embarrassed Annie, who initially did not join in jokingly, but instead offered only denials and groans. The fact that Annie liked the boy she was being teased about and may have had feelings of sexual attraction toward him may have contributed to her strong sense of embarrassment. Barbie and Ginny then mocked the notion of male sexual competence by having the boyfriend ask at one point, "Are we doin' it yet?" They then continued, by referring to a widely read novel called *Forever*, to make fun of beliefs that associate sexual experience with romantic love for women. This includes juxtaposing technical sexual phrases such as "in and out" with the romantic concept of "forever." This phrase is humorous because of the linking of romantic notions such as being in love "forever" with the mechanics of sexual intercourse, but also because it mocks the idea that romance must always be part of female sexuality. After the topic expanded to include a mocking of romance, Annie joined in by making fun of herself with a phrase that mocks the highly romantic portrayal of sexuality, saying, "If she seems to be cryin' it's a moment of joy!"[14]

It is interesting that Annie was able to join in the teasing once the topic broadened to include a mocking of romantic notions of female sexuality. These girls seem to have a shared sense of how romance is typically portrayed. Using humor to distance themselves from cultural beliefs about romance helps them to view themselves with humor even when they are the targets of teasing. In contrast, these girls appear to have less of a shared sense regarding the typical portrayal of sexuality. Although they are clearly challenging certain notions, such as the presumed greater competence of boys, they do not appear to be as detached from notions about female sexuality as they are from those about romantic beliefs.

Most of the examples of girls collectively resisting romantic and sexist messages occurred in groups of working-class girls. This may reflect the generally more rowdy and less inhibited style of girls in these groups. Since they tended to talk more freely about sexual themes, they may have been more comfortable including these themes in their collective teasing routines. Unfortunately, this did not mean these girls were necessarily less traditional in their future relations with boys. I [Cathy] was able to keep in contact with many of the girls from one of the medium-low-status groups through the rest of their teenage years and found out that several were raped during their first sexual encounter, while most of them had their first child as teenagers. This indicates that mocking romantic messages alone is not enough to alter current patterns of gender domination. It is essential that girls also challenge social messages about female sexuality and even more essential that boys also begin to modify their sexual attitudes.

The Larger Context of Romantic and Sexual Beliefs

The fact that romantic beliefs were challenged more than sexual beliefs may well reflect cultural processes in the larger society. In a study of media images, Angela McRobbie found that television romances now offer girls more alternatives by portraying scenarios in which girls can remain strong-minded and independent while in love. But McRobbie notes that, while there is now more open discussion of female sexuality through advice columns in teen magazines, the concerns still reflect an underlying double standard. For example, girls are given advice about what to do if he only wants sex or wants it sooner than she does, implying that his sexual needs are likely to be stronger or less controllable than her own.[15]

Public schools further reinforce the suppression of female desire through the lack of such discourse in sex education discussions. Michelle Fine found that the focus in these discussions was on girls as potential sexual victims—they were taught to defend themselves against disease, pregnancy, and "being used." While male desire is typically taught as being a normal biological process, through concepts such as "wet dreams" and "ejaculation," female desire is always tied to negative emotional, physical, moral, reproductive, and/or financial consequences. For example, when a girl asked about orgasms in one discussion, the topic shifted to better awareness of sexual disease. Fine concluded that a genuine discourse of desire would invite adolescents to explore what feels good and bad as well as to examine their own needs and limits. By doing so, girls would be "subjects of sexuality, initiators as well as negotiators."[16]

This double standard and the widespread use of negative sexual terms for adolescent girls is a powerful way of controlling their sexual assertiveness as well as their general life force. According to Audre Lorde, by controlling the life force of erotic energy you can control people.[17] Also, restricting the life force of women promotes an image of women as being passive sexually and dependent on men to initiate sexual activity. This image then becomes a societal justification for male sexual domination.[18]

Thus, while certain stereotypical feminine images are being challenged by some girls, the link between sexuality and gender inequality has not been challenged. According to Lorde, to do so would require a major transformation in our conception of the erotic. We need to disassociate the erotic from power as domination and begin to identify it with the powerful life forces within people such as their depth of feeling, sense of completeness, and feeling of internal satisfaction.[19] Societal messages about sexuality have focused on using people as objects of satisfaction or, as we have seen in this study, as objects for competition. Instead, erotic experiences could be ones that get people in touch with their deeper feelings. Expanding on this, Alice Walker has powerfully illustrated the importance of both men and women being sensitive to their partners' feelings as well their own in order to develop fuller, more complete sexual relationships.[20]

Currently, both boys and girls are being socialized to divert their attention away from inner feelings and their own sense of internal satisfaction. As long as boys focus on the goal of achieving a sexual encounter they will fail to be attuned to either their own feelings or those of their partner. Likewise, while girls are preoccupied with their external appearance, they cannot be fully aware of their own feelings and internal sense of satisfaction. Without access to the passion that arises from deeper levels of feelings, most male adolescents and many adults continue to associate excitement with a sense of domination and competition. Similarly, most girls fail to develop a sense of the depth of their inner resources and power and thus remain dominated and controlled. Finally, because stereotypical notions of sexuality are reflected in and constrained by the very language we use, new discourses will be needed to reflect an emergent consciousness of a more egalitarian sexuality.

9

Reconsidering Gender, Talk, and Inequality

Much of the early research on gender and language emphasized differences in the type of language activities and speech styles used by women as compared to men.[1] The focus of this book has been to expand our awareness of the importance of language by showing the central role that language plays in *constructing* cultural beliefs regarding gender. The findings of this study provide strong evidence of the importance of examining daily practices and language routines. Because language routines are recurrent and taken for granted, the beliefs they reflect often appear to be normative or natural views on gender. It is not until the language routines themselves are examined that the underlying beliefs are revealed as being simply a continual social construction. Furthermore, once these beliefs are revealed as cultural creations and not biological or concrete realities, it is possible to begin to challenge them openly to see if they reflect our sense of wholeness and justice.

The findings also support a dual view of language and power. Upon closer examination, the content of certain labels and insults represents a type of power that is constraining and limiting. For example, labels like *fag*, *wimp*, and *sissy* constrain the types of behaviors in which boys can engage, while other labels, such as *slut*, *whore*, and *dog*, limit girls' desires and sense of self. Some language routines also represent this type of power as routine, limiting options for alternative expressions. In addition, speech routines such as insult exchanges were used at times to ridicule lower-status students, thereby emphasizing power relations. More generally, insult exchanges were used and/or perceived as being a form of aggressive competition in which there was little concern for possible harm to others. The very structure of insult exchanges made it hard to challenge the negative assumption implicit in the labels being used. The structure of gossip also placed strong constraints on what could be expressed, making it very difficult to express disagreement unless one did so immediately.

Although language was often used to reinforce stereotypical notions of gender, a different type of power in language use was also evident—the power to create and transform meaning, thereby constructing new realities. All types of language routines offered some opportunities for self-expression. For most, considerable shaping of meaning occurred in the initial response. This was particularly true for insults and ridicule that could be transformed into more playful insult and teasing exchanges by responding in a nonserious manner. It was also true in gossip, since an initial response of disagreement could change the entire course of the gossip episode.

Some types of language routines offered greater flexibility for self-expression or the transformation of meaning. Collaborative stories allowed adolescents to present contrasting views about various gender beliefs, often showing how their own sense of sexual sophistication differed from those of significant adults in their lives. Teasing routines were often based on the mocking of cultural beliefs and included mocking many traditional views regarding appropriate feminine behavior. These routines offered opportunities for adolescents to *collectively* create their own beliefs regarding gender and sexuality, or at least to challenge existing ones.

The evidence of language use as a form of power that allows us to transform meaning and create new cultural beliefs reminds us of the importance of viewing language as an *active* force in cultural processes, and not simply as a reflection of existing beliefs. This understanding should encourage us to continue to examine the central role that language can play in working toward social change.

Gender Inequality

In this study, the central process we identified as promoting gender inequality was the objectification of girls. Both boys and girls at Woodview tended to focus their attention on external characteristics of girls, such as their physical attractiveness. In addition, boys typically perceived their female peers as passive sexual objects rather than as sexual actors in their own right. Other researchers have also viewed objectification as one of the central factors, if not the key factor, in the cultural beliefs that have sustained gender inequality over generations.

While standards regarding *what* is considered to be most beautiful change from decade to decade, beauty itself has remained a continual standard for evaluating femininity.[2] Some even argue that there is currently an increased focus on appearance as part of the backlash against women's advances in other areas.[3] Others who also see an increased concern with appearance believe it is due to an increase in advertisers' power over media as our culture becomes even more consumer oriented.[4] It is clear that this aspect of female oppression has been heavily internalized, with women's self-esteem tied strongly to their physical appearance. In fact, women who perceive their appearance to be inadequate claim that they suffer more from the continual disgrace of a "faulty" body part than they would from the process of altering that part through cosmetic surgery.[5]

The damage done to women by our culture's focus on appearance has received considerable criticism from feminists. Women who are evaluated primarily on the basis of being objects lose a sense of themselves as actors in the world. Even when they do develop some sense of agency through the knowledge that they can alter and "improve" their appearance,[6] they have less energy and time to invest in other aspects of self-definition.[7] This keeps their sense of worth attached to how they look rather than what they do. It also reduces the energy available for social change by failing to address the underlying problem of female objectification. Being viewed primarily as objects makes it easier for women to be the targets of other forms of abuse and mistreatment, since their full humanity is ignored.

Given that women are primarily judged by their appearance, it is not surprising that a second aspect of objectification is viewing women as sex objects rather than sexually active people. In previous decades, heterosexual relations strongly emphasized women as being passive and dependent on men. Within the sexual domain, women were expected to have fewer desires than men. They were also perceived to need men to awaken or develop their latent sexuality, which in turn reinforced the tendency to view men as sexual initiators and leaders.[8]

During the 1970s and 1980s, many people experimented with sexual liberation, attempting to overcome traditional attitudes and develop more egalitarianism between partners. Nonetheless, the double standard has remained intact. For example, sexual institutions such as prostitution are based on the belief that only men have sexual desires and that women are sexual servants. Within prostitution, men buy power in sexual exchange and thus continue to be sexually dominant, ordering women to fulfill their pleasures and fantasies.[9] Prostitution contributes to the general belief that it is normal and acceptable for men to be promiscuous, but that women are only openly sexual for economic gain or pathological reasons. Thus, only women in this culture are negatively labeled for having sexual desires. Sadly, the terms *slut* and *whore* are applied to girls as young as middle school age. Labeling young girls in this manner becomes part of a continual attempt to limit their sense of sexual autonomy and identity. Even adolescent victims of rape are often labeled sluts as if this is the only category for girls who have been involved in a sexual act.[10] This type of thinking furthers the belief that boys and men have the right to engage in sexual abuse as well as indiscriminate sexual behavior without being held accountable.

Girls and women continue to be viewed as sexual objects within the media as well as other arenas from cheerleading and pompom teams to swimsuit competitions. Increasingly, adult female models are portrayed as innocent and childlike in their sexual allure, while young girls are depicted as erotic and seductive.[11] Since girls are cast as sexual objects at such an early age, they often internalize this image as a central aspect of their identity. It then becomes extraordinarily difficult for them to move beyond this self-image to develop a greater sense of their own erotic potential as well as their general creative life force.[12] This denial contributes to such largely female maladies as anorexia and bulimia as well as a growing obsession with plastic surgery among adolescent girls.

Through objectification, women are denied their sense of totality. To be viewed primarily as a physical and sexual object is to experience denial of self as a whole person with thoughts, feelings, and actions.[13] Women must struggle to overcome a perception of self as object rather than subject before they can begin the process of self-definition as total and complete human beings. Only then can they develop their unique interests and have a real impact on the world around them. These findings also reveal some of the processes that contribute to men taking on dominating and oppressor roles in regard to women. To begin with, the boys in this study were encouraged to develop various aspects of toughness, including emotional invulnerability. Not only were they supposed to hide and control their own feelings, but they were also expected to act in ways that involved insensitivity to the feelings of others. Victor Seidler found that various forms of language, such as irony, disdain, and ritual insulting, are used by men to distance themselves from their ongoing emotional experiences. He sees this display of "coolness" as part of a general process of appearing self-controlled and able to manage one's feelings and desires.[14] Given the expectation that each person should manage his own feelings, it is not surprising that boys and men often stop attending to the feelings of others.

These findings also point to ways in which our society currently legitimizes male aggression. Although this aggression is supposed to be contained within a given "playing field" (such as sports arena, workplace, or battleground), it is so heavily tied to men's sense of masculinity that it pervades many aspects of their lives, including their sexual relationships. This legitimation of aggression, coupled with its close tie to masculinity, offers some explanation of why power and sexuality have become so intimately linked in this culture.

We must continue to examine the social processes of creating male oppressors. Until recently it was assumed by many that seeking power over others is a natural desire and thus not in need of explanation. However, there is now increasing awareness of belief systems and social institutions that cause people to take on the roles and behaviors of the oppressor as well as those of the oppressed.

While a competitive and hierarchal society appears on the surface to benefit those in powerful positions, a closer examination reveals that a competitive system does not necessarily meet the needs of people, even those with more status. To stay at the top of such a system, men are required to compete and prove themselves continually because their sense of worth and masculinity relies on external validation rather than an inner sense of self.[15] Low-status men must continually prove themselves as well. In doing so, men often forsake their creativity, full sexuality, intimate friendships, and general sense of caring.[16] By gaining a greater understanding of the processes that have created their role as oppressors, men will be better able to see what they have to gain by giving up this type of power.

The findings of this study show some of the important ways in which gender inequality is linked with other status processes. Because of the powerful social stratification at Woodview, being an isolate was highly feared. Further, isolates were often perceived to lack the very characteristics that represented rigid gender and sexual roles. To begin with, many isolates were labeled "fags" or "queers," adding to the strong pressure to be heterosexual. They were also ridiculed for being sissies if male or being ugly if female, promoting strong concerns with toughness and attractiveness, respectively. By associating the lowest social status in the school, the almost leperlike status of isolates, with qualities opposite those reflected in traditional gender roles, it became much more difficult for all of these adolescents to explore options beyond traditional and unequal heterosexual relationships.

10

Where Do We Go from Here?

In many ways, middle schools are microcosms of the larger society. Thus, the problems of gender inequality revealed in this study raise many important questions that deserve further reflection. To begin with, is it possible to reduce males' sexual power and aggressiveness while promoting aggressive competition in other areas of their lives? Can we teach adolescents that sexuality is about equal and intimate relationships, when the frameworks around them emphasize being dominant over others? Can we reduce sexual inequality without simultaneously reducing other forms of social inequality?

The findings of this study suggest that boys' aggressive and often insensitive treatment of girls stems directly from a more general focus on aggressive competition. They also suggest that fear of being different and fear of being at the bottom of a social hierarchy heighten boys' conformity to traditional masculine behavior,

157

indicating that general problems of social inequality will also need to be addressed for gender inequality ultimately to be eliminated.

Increasingly, we are faced with the realization that only broad-scale social change can address the problem of gender and sexual inequality. This includes a serious examination of our society's focus on aggressive competition. One action arising directly from the findings of this study would be to consider eliminating particularly aggressive and/or violent sports such as football and wrestling from secondary schools. These sports tie competition and ruthless aggression closely together and promote a violent orientation toward others in place of more creative forms of aggression. Schools could still offer other sports, such as track, gymnastics, and swimming, which provide boys and girls opportunities to succeed through a greater emphasis on self-challenge, competing against one's self and one's past record. Other school sports, such as volleyball, soccer, baseball, and basketball, none of which tie competition with violent or highly aggressive behavior, could provide opportunities for team involvement. Finally, if community members decide that their schools should include some outlets for aggressive energy, they could consider developing more creative outlets such as martial arts (which emphasize discipline and control) or certain forms of drama that would be available for girls as well as boys.

While some school districts might be able to consider such changes, many would face political pressure to maintain current athletic programs. However, we must begin to look more closely at the negative consequences of ruthlessly aggressive competition even if we are not yet ready for widespread modification of this basic value in American society. Currently, we are training young men to hurt others in order to get ahead in life.[1] It should be noted that this is not a mode of competition based strictly on self-betterment in which youth are being encouraged to compete with their own previous level of accomplishment either through individual or team effort. Instead it is a mode in which they are encouraged to ignore the harm they do to others as they take on the tasks of life. Young men are currently being taught to believe that people must look out for themselves without having concern for the welfare of others.

Some might argue that this stance has an important advantage of freeing energy by not requiring individuals to control aggression through concern for others. They might further argue that our ultimate success as a society requires this level of aggressive energy, given a need to compete with other highly competitive countries in a more global economy. According to them, this stance is not only good for people, but also is necessary for American success.

This thinking needs to be challenged and examined further. At some point, we as a society have to consider what our ultimate goals are and how we want to influence our youth in light of these goals. Is it truly our goal to be on top as a society at whatever cost to the welfare of others and to promote a worldwide system of aggressive competition in which everyone must continually struggle to get whatever piece of the pie they can? Or is it our goal to promote a world where most people enjoy a sense of well-being without endangering the welfare of others?

At this point, our belief in aggressive competition may be so strongly established that no other way even seems possible. In fact, many people fear their well-being will be hurt unless they can continue to compete in this manner.[2] But again, this type of belief requires greater reflection on what is necessary for our well-being and happiness. Since middle schools such as Woodview, as well as other school and work environments, tend to foster a sense of insecurity, most people do not look within themselves to discover sources of internal satisfaction. Instead, they seek well-being externally through social standing, material rewards, and recognition from others. Until this pattern is changed and people begin to discover sources of well-being within themselves, it is likely that we will continue to rely on competition that involves harm to others as people pursue what they have been led to believe is necessary for their happiness.[3]

The findings from this study also strongly indicate that activities like cheerleading and pompom teams, with their focus on appearance and attractiveness, are not in the best interest of our female youth. Some school districts may be able to eliminate these activities from their schools, but others are likely to encounter strong opposition, since it removes an opportunity for some girls to obtain status over others. Others might argue that since these pressures are already found in many forms of media, it makes no difference if certain school activities also promote a focus on female appearance.

Again, it is important to examine the meaning these activities provide for adolescents. Although only a small number of girls participate in such events, they focus the attention of the entire student body as well as audiences at athletic events on girls as objects to be seen. Unlike the athletes themselves, who are there to achieve and accomplish certain goals, these girls serve mainly as objects of adornment for athletic events.[4] And because these girls are primarily there to be gazed upon, they need to be pleasing to see. Thus, cheerleading activities contribute directly to focusing girls' success on superficial criteria—their physical selves.

Some might argue that attractiveness and beauty are admirable qualities and should be valued. However, in this society beauty is defined in limited ways that often exclude whole groups of women—for example, overweight women, women with rougher features, older women, and women of color. By focusing so much on outer appearance, much more meaningful aspects of beauty are often ignored. For example, according to Paula Gunn Allen, the brilliance of aging women is a form of beauty that is no longer seen by most white people in this society.[5] Also, the beauty of women who know how to create harmony among diverse groups of people has been advocated as a more important form of beauty than one's external image.[6] Many other valuable qualities are minimized or completely ignored in a society such as ours, which places so much attention on outward attractiveness. Of course, this type of beauty is more subject to external pressures. The cosmetic industry can't claim to provide changes in inner qualities, but people seek what it can offer them, to the ultimate limiting of their sense of self.

To get beyond these external pressures we would again need to look more inwardly for our own sense of beauty and appreciation. What is it that we actually appreciate most in ourselves and in others? Is it physical appearance, or is it something deeper, our sense of who we are as people—the wisdom gained over many years, the qualities we've developed to bring out the best in ourselves and in others, the ways in which we find commonalities across our many differences? All these offer a much more complete and ultimately satisfying sense of self than the more limited one fostered by cosmetic, and now cosmetic surgery, industries.

More Immediate Responses to Gender Inequality

Given the widespread nature of these changes, it is clear they will not be made overnight. Although it is crucial to continue to examine beliefs that underlie our current system, it is also important to monitor the pervasive harmful effects of this system. By supporting activities such as aggressive sports, schools, along with many other institutions, are contributing to gender and sexual inequality. Furthermore, these practices are often harmful to boys who are berated by coaches and male peers if they don't fit the "tough" masculine image. We as a society have a responsibility to those who may be harmed by our current cultural beliefs and practices.

Both girls and boys need to have more forums available, either in schools or elsewhere, where they can discuss how sexism and a limited view of femininity and masculinity directly affect their lives. Specifically, girls should be informed that some boys' athletic activities promote competitive aggression that which may carry over into their relationships with them and result in being treated primarily as sexual achievements or conquests. Girls also need to be alerted to the dangers of being objectified in general, to be shown how their own preoccupation with appearance keeps them focused on themselves as physical objects rather than as whole, complex people. They should be alerted to the messages all around them and especially those embedded in such salient school activities as cheerleading, pompom teams, or homecoming court selections. This greater awareness could even begin to foster some rebellion against these limiting roles.

Girls should also learn about the constraints of language—how words such as *slut, whore, virgin*, and *frigid* keep women locked into impossibly confining roles. These terms developed out of fear of women's power and erotic potential, but they continue to reflect this fear and to limit women's sexual experience and sense of power. Language can also create new realities, however. It is important for positive labels for women's sexual nature to be created and restored—for example, by drawing on the images of some female blues singers.[7]

Girls need to be assured that the ability to experience erotic feelings is not negative and does not reflect "loose morals" or deviant behavior. Instead, such a capacity reflects an ability to be in touch with deeper feelings and the power and intensity that arise when they are shared. Rather than encouraging girls to become pleasing sexual objects, we should encourage them to recognize and act on feelings that reflect a deeper sense of identity and satisfaction.

Although attempts should be made to reduce the sexual harassment and sexist insulting girls currently face in public schools, girls must also develop more techniques for dealing with such behavior. Obvious strategies such as teaching girls to state what they find offensive may not work. Girls say that they benefit from being encouraged to be more assertive, but some report that explicitly stating that someone is violating their rights often results in being laughed at and can lead to further ridicule. As one fourteen-year-old put it, "The last thing you can expect to get from boys is respect, because they don't respect themselves. The best you can do is confuse them."

Learning how to use language to transform the meaning of sexist comments is likely to be more effective. It is one way in which the power of language can be used to girls' advantage. This can be done, for example, by making an even more ridiculous or humorous comment, turning the humor back on the initial insulter, or finding ways to transform the meaning of an act or comment into a nonsexual domain. For example, an adolescent female described to me [Donna] an incident in which some boys harassed her and a girlfriend by making lewd pelvis thrusts. She and her friend playfully turned the meaning of their movements into inept attempts at skiing. In another example, based on the strategy of confusing boys rather than trying to gain their respect, one girl said that she would respond to boys' insults with "psychobabble," asking questions such as "Do you need mental health?" or "Why do you feel a need to express your turmoil by being aggressive to people you don't know?"

Girls also need more adults who take the issue of sexual harassment seriously and are prepared to deal with it effectively.[8] Too often the male officials to whom girls report incidents are well-meaning but ineffective. In one case, a boy who had been harassing a girl near her locker was punished by being made her "protector" for the rest of the year. After he was instructed to stand by her locker and see that no one else bullied her, she reported finding even more ways to avoid going to her locker than she had before.

Girls should have available more adults, whether school counselors or principals, trained in problems of sexual harassment. They also need forums where feminist topics and issues are treated seriously, as well as more curricular focus on strong, successful women leaders, writers, artists, and scientists. While some girls report having discussions about feminist issues on their own, they often face various stigmas associated with feminism and are ridiculed for being lesbian or too "bookish." It is important, therefore, that adults promote opportunities for this type of dialogue to occur.

Boys also need forums in which issues of masculinity and sexuality are directly addressed. Currently, schools set up a framework that often legitimizes verbal and physical abuse by certain boys toward other boys. One man described a practice in which his physical education teacher required nonathletes to do favors for the boys who were on the key athletic teams, setting up a system of male-to-male dominance and subservience. He reported that coaches and male teachers assumed that the athletes would further their dominance by active physical and verbal harassment during lunchtime, and they did little to intervene when this occurred. In this study we saw how male peers imitated the behavior of their coaches, berating boys for not continuing to play despite a serious injury.

Boys who wish to try out for different activities or adopt nonstereotypical roles are often ridiculed by their male peers. For example, one eighth-grade boy who decided he wanted to challenge the idea that only girls could be cheerleaders was the first boy in his school to join the cheerleading squad. Even though he had also been on the football team that year, he was ridiculed by his male classmates who called him "cheerleader," "wussy boy," and "faggot." He explained that the ridicule stopped when his female friends on the cheerleading team came to his defense and told these boys "Hey, it's cool. Leave him alone."

In general, boys as well as girls need support for being individuals and for being different from their peers if they choose to be. The boy who became a cheerleader reported, "I like being different. I don't want to be part of a crowd. It's cool to be different." Schools like Harmony, an alternative school with grades kindergarten through twelfth, are able to support the idea of being different, in part because smaller schools allow more opportunity for being known as individuals. An eighth-grade boy who attends Harmony said that students there often end up mocking people who conform to certain roles, including the traditional masculine role. One way this happens is by saying, "I'm so cool," while pretending to act and look tough. Boys in public schools also need opportunities to explore their individual interests and ways of expressing themselves. School officials can help to promote the idea that being different can be positive, not negative.

Boys need to be shown models for sexual behavior that do not rely on a competitive framework. This is not simply an issue of teaching them responsible sexual behavior—it is a matter of encouraging them to view erotic connections as a form of true communication. Like girls, boys should be encouraged to examine their daily language routines to see if they mean to convey the potentially sexist messages they often imply. Since many acts of prejudice occur because people are unaware of the potentially racist, sexist, or heterosexist nature of a remark, it is important that boys both find out how others interpret their comments and have occasions to explore different potential meanings among themselves.

In addition, boys and girls would both benefit from joint discussions about modes of intimacy and male-female relationships that go beyond stereotypical roles. Such open discussions would help them identify common concerns and feelings that unite them despite their differences. These could take place in social studies courses or during homeroom meetings, which are used in many schools as occasions for students to discuss ongoing social and interpersonal concerns.

Finally, boys and girls need more opportunities to relate to each other as equal, whole people. The extent to which differences exist between girls and boys is beyond the scope of this book, but it is essential that any differences that do exist not be the basis for inequality.[9] To promote more equal relationships between girls and boys it is essential that they have many opportunities to work and play together. Barrie Thorne offers many suggestions regarding the need for cooperative learning situations that could bring boys and girls together in the classroom.[10] In addition, more of the activities offered in secondary schools should be mixed-gender. This might mean having a wider range of intramural sports where the focus is on participating and having fun rather than on winning. It could also include offering a wider range of clubs and nonathletic activities at the middle school level. Joint participation in such activities should increase opportunities for cross-sex friendships, which offer one of the best models for egalitarian relationships.

Addressing the Problems of Social Rankings Within Schools

Attempts need to be made to reduce the extent of social ranking within middle schools. Having only a few extracurricular activities that give a small number of students visibility promotes a sense of insecurity for many. Since most students value being known by others and being recognized in some way, schools should be changed to make this more possible.

Some districts have eliminated extracurricular activities at the middle school level. This ameliorates the problem of creating a handful of elite students but does not address the issue of making students feel that they are known by others. Other middle schools have taken stronger steps by not only eliminating competitive extracurricular activities but also creating smaller "schools" within a single large school building. Realizing that students often do better socially and academically in smaller school environments, these schools have returned to the concept of dividing into smaller units within well-equipped large facilities. These smaller "schools" are entirely self-contained in that students only interact with other youth and teachers within their "school" and do not have any large school events. In this environment, it is not that difficult for all students to be known by others in their "school."

Harmony School has taken this a step further.[11] At the end of each year, each student is recognized for at least one way in which she or he stood out or improved significantly. In the first two grades, these accomplishments and talents are identified by teachers. After that, other students help to identify them. Thus, in this school, all students receive special recognition from their teachers and their peers.

These types of major changes in school programming and structure are needed to address the problems of social rankings within schools. Until they are introduced, students are likely to continue to be insecure and unwilling to develop individual styles that deviate from social class and gender norms. In addition, some youths are likely to continue to be the target of others' insecurity through the extensive practice of ridicule and even physical abuse.

Until these changes are in place and even after they are introduced, students will also need other forums and avenues for addressing the problems of student ridicule and conflict. Harmony School and some other alternative schools have regular family meetings in which students are encouraged to make decisions and choices about their school as well as to discuss problems. Through these discussions they gain conflict-resolution skills and learn how to have greater empathy for the feelings of others. With these forums available, students are less likely to be cast into isolate roles year after year.[12]

Recently, concerned adults in our local community have started a student action group called KACTIS—Kids Against Cruel Treatment in Schools. This after-school group brings together students from different elementary schools to talk about the problem of ridiculing others and engaging in other forms of cruelty. Initially, it provided them with an opportunity to talk about acts of cruel treatment they had either experienced or witnessed. In these discussions and early attempts at role-play, students revealed their lack of skills for dealing with conflicts and expressing anger. During the program's second year, specific strategies for conflict resolution and assertive expression of anger were introduced. Students were then encouraged to incorporate these skills when role-playing to arrive at new strategies for dealing with conflict and for confronting students who were ridiculing or harassing others.

In working with this group and from conducting this study, it is clear that certain alternative strategies are likely to be more effective than others. Students are sometimes resistant to learning ways to be "nicer" to their peers, but an important component of student peer culture is humor—being able to get others to laugh. Being able to respond in a playful or lighthearted manner is important when students are being insulted or teased. An insult routine involves another insult as a response, but the teasing routine involves a range of playful responses. However, since the response is what brings out the meaning of the initial remark, even insults can be responded to in other, playful ways and turned into the less competitive activity of teasing. One of the best illustrations we observed of this strategy occurred during a volleyball practice at Woodview one day. During the course of some other teasing, someone commented on another team member's revealing outfit.

> They were kidding Sylvia for a while about her name and various things. Then at one point Rita said, "Sylvia's showing off her bra with her white T-shirt," referring to the fact that you could see her bra through her T-shirt. Sylvia wasn't insulted or hurt. Instead, she lifted up her shirt and said, "When I show off my bra, I'll do it like this!" [Donna's notes]

While Sylvia could easily have taken Rita's insult seriously, rather than become angry or respond with a counter insult, she chose to respond by making fun of herself. By turning the activity into one of playful teasing she showed that she didn't regard the accusation of being a showoff seriously. In addition, this humorous response made everyone laugh and helped defuse the tension which had begun to build.

By demonstrating one's ability to make humorous comments such as this, students show they have one of the most valuable skills in children's peer culture—the ability to make others laugh. In addition, by turning the humor on themselves rather than back toward the other person, they decrease the competitive tone of the interaction while also showing that they are able to not take themselves too seriously. As useful as this strategy is, it may be hard for students to come up with humorous comments about themselves right on the spot. KACTIS and similar programs can help by providing students with regular opportunities to develop creative and/or humorous responses to ridicule through popular activities such as role-play and dramatic skits.

Another way students can practice new responses is to intervene when others are being ridiculed. In this study we saw a number of intervention strategies. These included asking students not to be so rude, telling them they were making fools of themselves, and defending the student being challenged. The more students practice assertive and creative intervention skills in special programs like KACTIS or on the playground, the more options they have when they witness abuse or harassment on the part of another student. In one KACTIS role-playing episode, ridicule consisting of animal name-calling was converted by an intervener into a friendly competition over who could make the strangest animal noises. As with sexual harassment, the best strategy at times may be to confuse the ridiculer by switching to a completely different mode of talk. In addition to the "psychobabble" example given earlier, we as sociologists offer the option of adopting "sociobabble," saying, "Do you have any

169

more examples of your cultural knowledge that you would like to share with me?"[13]

Youth, to some, is a carefree time that comes before the responsibilities of work and family. Unfortunately, the reality of this period of life in many public schools is less a time to learn and to enjoy one's friends and more a time of figuring out how to avoid getting harassed on the way to your locker. Many people have asked, "Have incidents of ridicule and sexual harassment in schools increased in frequency or intensity?" There have been few studies of this nature in the past, so it is difficult to offer an answer other than what can be assessed from our collective memories. Most people claim that the talk of youth is more explicit now, due perhaps to greater exposure to media of all types and especially to movies. We do know that there is a greater incidence of violence of all types in schools and that students themselves report difficulty dealing with conflicts with peers. This suggests the need to respond actively to the issues raised in this study rather than assume that they are simply part of growing up.

We believe that changes in beliefs and policies are needed, but we also have repeatedly emphasized the power of language. Having identified some of the ways in which young people routinely use language to reinforce stereotypical views, we hope that the transformative power of language can serve more often as a means for challenging those views and providing youth with the opportunity to express their uniqueness and intervene on the behalf of others. We believe that some of the most successful strategies stem from reinforcing adolescents' own desire to be creative and engagingly humorous as they confront the day-to-day problems of school life.

APPENDIX
Notes on Methodology

From the beginning, this study involved a team approach to data collection. Since most school ethnographies have involved a single investigator, it is often hard to get a broad range of perspectives on students' experiences. While researchers have sometimes joined several groups, it still is difficult to capture the experiences of students from all gender, class, ethnic, and status levels within a given school.[1] For this reason, several research assistants were asked to join this project in order to examine adolescents' peer culture from a range of vantage points. Because much less was known about the experience of girls than boys in secondary schools, the initial focus of the study was on a detailed examination of their peer cultures at different class and status levels. Later, a male researcher was included on the project to focus on boys' experience in the same school.

Collecting Data on Students's Experiences

We used a variety of means to collect data on students' experiences with peers in school. All four researchers (Donna Eder, Cathy Evans, Steve Parker, and Stephanie Sanford) observed lunchtime interaction at least twice weekly for periods of time ranging from five months in Stephanie's case to twelve months in Donna's case. We never took notes openly during the lunch period, but sometimes recorded brief notes in the bathroom or hallway between lunch sessions. These notes were expanded upon and all notes were recorded fully immediatey after leaving the setting.

Donna Eder and Steve Parker also atended male and female extracurricular activities twice weekly for an entire academic year. Given the importance of athletic activities and cheerleading, we focused primarily on them, going to athletic games and practices, pep rallies, and cheerleading practices and tryouts. In addition, we observed choir and band practices and concerts, talent shows, and the one school play that was performed during the three-year period of the study. We were able to take some notes during these events, since our roles were more those of observers than participants. Afterward, we expanded on these notes and recorded them fully.

After all of our field notes were coded, the codes were entered onto a computer where word search programs could easily identify all cases of a particular code. This was essential for coordinating over one thousand pages of coded field notes that were recorded for this study.

Once we had been in the setting for several months, we began doing informal interviews with individuals or groups of students on issues that arose from our observations. They included questions about the meaning of popularity, attitudes toward other students in the school, and views on male-female relationships. While some were so informal they were simply recorded as field notes, ten of the more extensive interviews were tape-recorded and transcribed in full.

Finally, we tape-recorded conversations in most of the lunch groups which we observed.[2] Typically, we sat with the group members for three to seven months prior to taping them, so they were already used to our presence. We got written permission from both the students and their parents before we made a recording. On the permission forms we assured them that no one who knew them would be able to listen to or watch the tapes. We also told them that their real names would not be used in any written report. To further insure the participants' privacy, we have also changed all names of identifying locations and modified discussions about particular people or events. Only one parent requested that her daughter not participate in the study. Since she could not be asked to separate from her group, we decided to omit the entire group from the study.

We were able to capture the typical interactions of most of the girls' groups through audiotape recordings, but in the case of one female group and all of the male groups we found it necessary to videotape as well. These groups engaged in a lot of nonverbal behavior along with their verbal conversations and sometimes had several conversations at once, which were difficult to transcribe without the aid of a video-recording. All of the audio-recordings took place right in the lunchroom. Since it would have created too much interest and chaos to bring the videocamera into the lunch room, we did the video-recordings in the media center, a room to which students were free to go to during lunchtime. At times students paid explicit attention to the tape recorder or camera, shouting humorous remarks into the microphone or showing their muscles to the camera. Much of the time they continued to interact as they would normally have done, however. In particular, they were just as likely to gossip, insult, tease, and tell stories when they were being recorded as they were on other days, since these routines were so much a part of their daily interactions.[3]

173

The researchers involved in data collection and coding met, along with four other project assistants, on a regular basis throughout the three-year study. We used these group meetings to share information about what we were observing as well as to compare interpretations of key events and activities. This proved an extremely important part of the project, allowing us to continually refine our understanding of peer concerns and styles of interaction. It was particularly important to have both "insider" and "outsider" perspectives on gender-related behavior. For example, Steve was not at all surprised by the coaches' behavior during practices or by the boys' aggressive style at lunch, believing that he was finding "nothing new." However, all of the females on the project were surprised by the high degree of aggressiveness promoted by both the coaches and adolescent males, seeing it as a strong contrast to our own experiences as adolescent females as well as a contrast to most of the girls in the study. At the same time, because Steve was male he was not only able to develop a strong rapport with the male students, but he also provided important interpretations of ritual insulting and the effect of different types of responses.

Ethical Issues

When we first began the study, we openly informed all of the students that we were from Indiana University and were doing a study of middle school students. We assured students of our concern with protecting their privacy by not using their actual names or revealing private information to others who might know them. The only concern expressed by a few students was that they not get in trouble for swearing. Since we were not aware of a no-swearing rule and had not been asked to enforce it, they soon lost this concern. Several students again expressed a similar concern when they were first tape-recorded, asking us who would be allowed to hear the tapes. We assured them that the tapes would not be seen or heard by anyone who could identify them and that we would not use their names in papers or books about the study.

We were prepared in advance for these particular ethical issues and had ready responses that relieved people's concerns. Other ethical dilemmas arose during the course of the study for which we did not have clear solutions. Both Steve and Cathy witnessed several incidents of verbal harassment, and Steve witnessed one incident that included physical harassment. Since we had tried from the start to minimize our roles as authority figures in the school, neither of them intervened as adults to stop these incidents. Instead they relied on nonintrusive strategies such as not participating themselves, or drawing the attention of others away from the target of ridicule to some other activity.

These incidents raise challenging questions about the role of researchers as observers of naturally occurring behavior, as opposed to interventionists who try to change the behavior of others, especially if it appears to be cruel or abusive. Had we decided to intervene more directly, we would have been seen as authority figures, and it is likely that students would no longer have acted as naturally in our presence, thus limiting cne extent to which we could gain information about peer interactions. On the other hand, it was deeply disturbing to the researchers to witness these events without intervening. We struggled with the question of whether nonintervention might convey an implicit message that such behavior is acceptable to adults.

Although we were not able to resolve this dilemma during the course of our study, we believe that it is an important one that deserves more discussion by those engaged in field work. At the same time, we have felt a strong responsibility for making others more aware of the problems that students, especially isolates, currently face in school settings. We hope this study will increase people's awareness of this important social problem.[4]

Notes

2. *Gender, Talk, and School Culture*

1. See also Alexandra Dundas Todd and Sue Fisher, "Theories of Gender, Theories of Discourse," in *Gender and Discourse: The Power of Talk*, ed. A. Todd and S. Fisher (Norwood, N.J.: Ablex, 1988), 1–18; Ellen Messner-Davidow, "Know-How," in *(En)Gendering Knowledge: Feminists in Academe* (Knoxville: University of Tennessee Press, 1991), 281–310.

2. See also William Corsaro, "Interpretive Reproduction in Children's Peer Cultures," *Social Psychology Quarterly* 55 (1992): 160–177; William Corsaro and Donna Eder, "Children's Peer Cultures," *Annual Review of Sociology* 16 (199): 197–220; Barrie Thorne, *Gender Play: Boys and Girls in School* (New Brunswick, N.J.: Rutgers University Press, 1993).

3. Anthony Giddens, *The Constitution of Society* (Oxford: Polity Press, 1984); William Corsaro and Donna Eder, "The Development and

Socialization of Children and Adolescents," in *Socialization Perspectives on Social Psychology*, ed. K. Cook, G. Fine, and J. House (New York: Allen and Bacon, 1994).

4. Erving Goffman, *Frame Analysis* (New York: Harper & Row, 1974).

5. Corsaro and Eder, "The Development and Socialization of Children and Adolescents."

6. Thorne, *Gender Play*.

7. William Corsaro, *Friendship and Peer Culture in the Early Years* (Norwood, N.J.: Ablex, 1985); William Corsaro, "Routines in the Peer Culture of American and Italian Nursery School Children," *Sociology of Education* 61 (1988): 1–14; William Corsaro and Thomas Rizzo, "*Discussione* and Friendship: Socialization Processes in the Peer Culture of Italian Nursery School Children," *American Sociological Review* 53 (1988): 879–894.

8. Marjorie Goodwin, *He-Said-She-Said: Talk as Social Organization among Black Children* (Bloomington: Indiana University Press, 1990). We will use different terms to refer to racial and ethnic differences. The terms *black* and *white* will be used when referring to previous studies that use these terms and when race is being highlighted. Otherwise we will use the terms *Euro-American* and *Afro-American* to emphasize that all people have an ethnic heritage. (We find these terms less formal and cumbersome than *European-American* and *African-American*.)

9. David Maltz and Ruth Borker, "A Cultural Approach to Male-Female Miscommunication," in *Language and Social Identity*, ed. John Gumperz (New York: Cambridge University Press, 1983), 105–216; Deborah Tannen, *You Just Don't Understand: Women and Men in Conversation* (New York: Morrow, 1990).

10. See also Thorne, *Gender Play*.

11. Robert Connell, *Gender and Power* (Stanford: Stanford University Press, 1987); Thorne, *Gender Play*.

12. Nancy Henley, *Body Politics: Power, Sex, and Nonverbal Communication* (Englewood, N.J.: Prentice-Hall, 1977).

13. Sue Lees, *Losing Out: Sexuality and Adolescent Girls* (London: Hutchinson, 1986); Cathy Evans and Donna Eder, " 'No Exit': Processes of Social Isolation in the Middle School," *Journal of Contemporary Ethnography* 22 (1993): 139–170.

14. R. Coward and J. Ellis, *Language and Materialism: Developments in Semiology and the Theory of the Subject* (London: Routledge and Kegan Paul, 1977); Dale Spender, *Man Made Language* (London: Routledge and

Kegan Paul, 1980); Todd and Fisher, "Theories of Gender, Theories of Discourse, 1–18; Sue Lees, *Sugar and Spice: Sexuality and Adolescent Girls* (London: Penguin Books, 1993).

15. Hugh Mehan, *Learning Lessons* (Harvard: Harvard University Press, 1979); Sue Fisher and Alexandra Todd, *Discourse and Institutional Authority: Medicine, Education and Law* (Norwood, N.J.: Ablex, 1986); Goffman, *Frame Analysis*.

16. Spender, *Man Made Language*.

17. Lees, *Sugar and Spice*. *Slag* is a British term, referring to females who are viewed as sexually promiscuous or as deviant in some other way. It comes from the belief that, like the leftover slag after mining, these girls are also "leftovers"—no longer virgin.

18. Coward and Ellis, *Language and Materialism*.

19. Hazel Carby, "It Jus Be's Dat Way Sometime: The Sexual Politics of Women's Blues," in *Gender and Discourse: The Power of Talk*, ed. Todd and Fisher, 227–242; Patricia Hill Collins, *Black Feminist Thought: Knowledge, Consciousness, and the Politics of Empowerment* (New York: Routledge, 1990); Gloria Anzuldua, "La Conciencia de la Mestiza: Towards a New Consciousness," in *Making Face, Making Soul: Haciendo Caras*, ed. G. Anzuldua (San Francisco: Aunt Lute Foundation, 1990), 377–389; Laura Coltelli, *Winged Words: American Indian Writers Speak* (Lincoln: University of Nebraska Press, 1990).

20. Todd and Fisher, "Theories of Gender, Theories of Discourse."

21. Coward and Ellis, *Language and Materialism*.

22. Helena Wulff, *Twenty Girls: Growing Up, Ethnicity, and Excitement in a South London Microculture*, Stockholm Studies in Social Anthropology, no. 21. (Stockholm, Sweden: University of Stockholm, 1988).

23. Thorne, *Gender Play*.

24. Janet Schofield, *Black and White in School* (New York: Praeger, 1982); Raphela Best, *We've All Got Scars* (Bloomington: Indiana University Press, 1983); Thorne, *Gender Play*.

25. Goodwin, *He-Said-She-Said*.

26. James Coleman, *The Adolescent Society* (New York: Free Press, 1961).

27. Denise Kandel and Gerald Lesser, *Youth in Two Worlds* (San Francisco: Jossey-Bass, 1972).

28. Coleman, *The Adolescent Society*; Philip Cusick, *Inside High School* (New York: Holt, Rinehart, and Winston, 1973); Penelope Eckert, *Jocks and Burnouts: Social Categories and Identity in the High School*

(New York: Teachers College Press, 1989); Nancy Lesko, *Symbolizing Society: Stories, Rites and Structure in Catholic High School* (Philadelphia: Falmer, 1988).

29. Cusick, *Inside High School;* Joyce Canaan, "A Comparative Analysis of American Suburban Middle Class, Middle School, and High School Teenage Culture," in *Interpretative Ethnography of Education: At Home and Abroad* (Hillsdale, N.J.: Lawrence Erlbaum Associates, 1987), 385–408; Eckert, *Jocks and Burnouts;* D. Eder and D. Kinney, "The Effect of Middle School Extracurricular Activities on Adolescents' Populari and Peer Status," *Youth and Society* 26 (1995): 298–324.

30. Eckert, *Jocks and Burnouts.*

31. Ibid.; Lesko, *Symbolizing Society;* J. MacLeod, *Ain't No Maki. It: Leveled Aspirations in a Low-Income Neighborhood* (Boulder, Colo.: Wesi view Press, 1987).

32. Canaan, "A Comparative Analysis of American Suburba Middle Class, Middle School, and High School Teenage Culture, 385–408. Junior high schools typically begin in seventh grade, whil most middle schools start a grade or two earlier. The main differenc between the two terms, however, is that middle school is a more recent term for a middle-grade-level school. Some middle schools now also begin in seventh grade and are similar in programming and structure to former junior high schools. We will use the term that was used at the time the research was conducted in referring to these schools.

33. Roberta Simmons and Dale Blyth, *Moving into Adolescence: The Impact of Pubertal Change and School Context* (New York: Aldine de Gruyter, 1987).

34. David Kinney, "From 'Nerds' to 'Normals': Adolescent Identity Recovery within a Changing School Social System," *Sociology of Education* 66 (1993):21–40.

35. See also Canaan, "A Comparative Analysis of American Suburban Middle Class, Middle School, and High School Teenage Culture."

36. Simmons and Blyth, *Moving into Adolescence.*

37. Schofield, *Black and White in School;* W. Shrum, N. Cheek, and S. Hunter, "Friendship in School: Gender and Racial Homophily," *Sociology of Education* 61 (1988): 227–239.

38. Best, *We've All Got Scars;* Thorne, *Gender Play;* Patricia Adler, Steven Kless, and Peter Adler, "Socialization to Gender Roles: Elementary School Boys and Girls," *Sociology of Education* 65 (1992): 169–187.

39. Adler, Kless, and Adler, "Socialization to Gender Roles."

40. Paul Willis, *Learning to Labour* (New York: Columbia Univer-

sity Press, 1981); Joyce Ladner, *Tomorrow's Tomorrow* (Garden City, N.Y.: Doubleday, 1972); Angela McRobbie, "Working Class Girls and the Culture of Femininity," in *Women Take Issue*, ed. Women's Studies Group, Center for Contemporary Cultural Studies (University of Birmingham, London: Hutchinson, 1978), 96–108; Christine Griffin, *Typical Girls?: Young Women from School to the Job Market* (London: Routledge, 1985).

41. R. Connell et al., *Making the Difference: Schools, Families, and Social Division* (Sydney: Allen and Unwin, 1982); S. Kessler, D. Ashenden, R. Connell, and G. Dowsett, "Gender Relations in Secondary Schooling," *Sociology of Education* 58 (1985): 34–47. This study did not find extracurricular activities to be as central in developing a predominant form of femininity, perhaps because cheerleading and pompom teams do not exist in Australian schools.

42. Joyce Canaan, "Passing Notes and Telling Jokes: Gendered Strategies Among American Middle School Teenagers," in *Uncertain Terms: Negotiating Gender in American Culture*, ed. Faye Ginsburg and Anna Lowenhaupt Tsing (Boston: Beacon Press, 1991), 215–231.

43. Barrie Thorne and Zella Luria, "Sexuality and Gender in Children's Daily Worlds," *Social Problems* 33 (1986): 176–189; Thorne, *Gender Play*.

44. Lees, *Losing Out*.

45. Gary Fine, *With the Boys: Little League Baseball and Preadolescent Culture* (Chicago: University of Chicago Press, 1987).

46. Willis, *Learning to Labour*.

47. See the following references if you are interested in other aspects of adolescent peer culture that were not necessarily related to the theme of gender inequality: Donna Eder, "The Cycle of Popularity: Interpersonal Relations Among Female Adolescents," *Sociology of Education* 58 (1985): 154–165; Donna Eder, "Building Cohesion Through Collaborative Narration," *Social Psychology Quarterly* 35 (1988); Donna Eder, "The Role of Teasing in Adolescent Peer Culture," in *Sociological Studies of Child Development*, vol. 4, ed. S. Cahill (Greenwich, Conn.: JAI Press, 1991), 181–197; Donna Eder and Janet Enke, "The Structure of Gossip: Opportunities and Constraints on Collective Expression Among Adolescents," *American Sociological Review* 56 (1991): 495–508; Donna Eder and Stephan Sanford, "The Development and Maintenance of Interactional Norms Among Early Adolescents," in *Sociological Studies of Child Development*, vol. 1, ed. P. Adler and P. Adler (Greenwich, Conn.: JAI Press, 1986), 283–300; Stephen Parker, "Early

Adolescent Male Cultures: The Importance of Organized and Informal Sport" (Ph.D. diss., Indiana University, 1991); Robin Simon, Donna Eder, and Cathy Evans, "The Development of Feeling Norms Underlying Romantic Love Among Adolescent Females," *Social Psychology Quarterly* 55 (1992): 29–46.

48. One person who transcribed our audiotapes of girls engaging in ritual insulting assumed that the girls were Afro-American when in fact most were Euro-American.

49. Donna Eder, " 'Go Get Ya a French!': Romantic and Sexual Teasing Among Adolescent Girls," in *Gender and Conversational Interaction*, ed. Deborah Tannen (New York: Oxford University Press, 1993), 17–31.

50. Parker, "Early Adolescent Male Cultures."

51. Adler, Kless, and Adler, "Socialization to Gender Roles"; Thorne, *Gender Play*.

52. Connell et al., *Making the Difference:* Dorothy Holland and Margaret Eisenhart, *Educated in Romance: Women, Achievement, and College Culture* (Chicago: University of Chicago Press, 1990).

3. *Entering the World of Middle School*

1. My own discomfort with having difficulty joining an eighth-grade group provides evidence of how powerful the nature of cliques can be at this grade level.

2. Throughout, we will use the grade level of most group members when referring to a group by grade level.

3. All student names and locations used throughout the text are pseudonyms; researchers' real names are used.

4. We defined group membership based on the number of students who sat with the group for at least a month. The membership varied for many groups over the course of the year, and, for those studied over two or more years, there were additional changes in membership.

5. Although the terms *high, medium-high, medium-low,* and *low* reflect the overall perspective of the school status rankings, students' perspectives varied depending on the status position of their group. For example, students on the high-status side of the cafeteria referred to all

of the students on the other side as "grits," but most of the students on the low-status side used the label *grits* for a few students or groups they perceived to be of lower status than themselves. Likewise, students in some of the medium-low-status groups were perceived as being very popular by other students on the lower-status side of the cafeteria, while students on the high status side would not have considered them popular at all.

6. For more on this critique, see Thorne, *Gender Play*.

7. For each group we will refer to one or more of the most visible members to help familiarize readers with some of the students' names used in examples throughout the book. In some cases these individuals played clear leadership roles, while in others they were the center of other group members' attention.

8. Thorne, in *Gender Play*, found that "going with" someone was a central activity by fifth and sixth grade and was similar in nature to the activity described here.

4. Segregating the Unpopular from the Popular

1. Canaan, "A Comparative Analysis of American Suburban Middle Class, Middle School, and High School Teenage Culture," 385–408.

2. Some males reported that they were not going out for certain sports activities because they lacked interest, not skill, in them. For example, one boy said that he wasn't going to go out for wrestling because he didn't like the way it made him feel—after wrestling someone he would often feel like vomiting.

3. Eder, "The Cycle of Popularity."

4. All transcribed excerpts are from naturally occurring conversations during lunch unless noted as being part of an informal interview with students. When transcribing our tapes there were cases in which we were not completely sure of the word or words being spoken but could make a reasonable guess. These are noted in the transcripts by the phrase "less audible" immediately following the word or words. If an entire sentence was less audible this is noted as well.

5. Eder, "They Cycle of Popularity."

6. For an excellent analysis of the relationship between social class and social status in school see Ellen Brantlinger, *The Politics of Social Class in Secondary School* (New York: Teachers College Press, 1993).

7. Each week a different group of students was assigned to clean-up duty in the cafeteria. Within this group some were asked to clean the tables on one side of the cafeteria, while others were asked to clean the other side.

8. The students on the low-status side of the cafeteria tended to wear older clothes and spend less time fixing their hair, but they did not have a different degree of cleanliness. It is possible that students associate older clothes and less stylish hair with a lower degree of cleanliness.

9. Brantlinger, *Social Class.*

10. On this particular day the only boy in the group wearing a Polo-brand shirt was Joe, not Mike, and Mike was no more likely to wear designer clothes than any of the other group members.

11. Although racist jokes and comments were not heard at all in several of the groups, they were occasionally heard in other male groups and in some of the female groups. In a few cases the students seemed embarrassed by making such remarks in front of an adult, something that never occurred with sexist remarks. This suggests that our presence may have influenced the frequency of racist comments on the part of at least some students.

12. Evans and Eder, " 'No Exit.' "

13. Ibid

14. Ibid.

15. J. D. and K. A. Dodge, "Multiple Sources of Data on Social Behavior and Social Status in the School: A Cross-age Comparison," *Child Development* 59 (1988): 815–829; J. D. Coie and K. A. Dodge, "Continuities and Changes in Children's Social Status: A Five-year Longitudinal Study," *Merrill-Palmer Quarterly* 29 (1983): 261–282.

16. Evans and Eder, " 'No Exit.' "

17. S. Oden and S. R. Asher, "Coaching Children in Social Skills for Friendship Making," *Child Development* 48 (1977): 495–506.

18. Thomas J. Berndt, "Correlates and Causes of Sociometric Status in Childhood: A Commentary on Six Current Studies of Popular, Rejected, and Neglected Children," *Merrill-Palmer Quarterly* 29(4) (1983): 439–448; Dale A. Blyth, "Surviving and Thriving in the Social World: A Commentary on Six New Studies of Popular, Rejected, and Neglected Children," *Merrill-Palmer Quarterly* 29(4) (1983): 449–458.

19. J. Gottlieb and M. Budoff, "Social Acceptability of Retarded

Children in Nongraded Schools Differing in Architecture," *American Journal of Mental Deficiency* 78 (1973): 15–19.

20. B. F. Perlmutter, J. Crocker, D. Corray, and D. Garstecki, "Sociometric Status and Related Personality Characteristics of Main-streamed Learning Disabled Adolescents," *Learning Disability Quarterly* 6 (1983): 20–30.

21. M. T. Hallinan, "Friendship Patterns in Open and Traditional Classrooms," *Sociology of Education* 49 (1976): 254–265.

22. M. Ballard, L. Corman, J. Gottlieb, and M. Kaufman, "Improving the Social Status of Mainstreamed Retarded Children," *Journal of Educational Psychology* 69 (1977): 605–611.

23. Jesse Goodman, *Elementary Schooling for Critical Democracy* (Albany: State University of New York Press, 1992).

24. Canaan, "A Comparative Analysis of American Suburban Middle Class, Middle School, and High School Teenage Culture"; Kinney, "From 'Nerds' to 'Normals.' "

25. Canaan, "A Comparative Analysis of American Suburban Middle Class, Middle School, and High School Teenage Culture."

26. David Kinney, "Dweebs, Headbangers, and Trendies: Adolescent Identity Formation and Change within Socio-Cultural Contexts" (Ph.D. thesis, Indiana University, 1990).

27. Willis, *Learning to Labour.*

5. Tough Guys, Wimps, and Weenies

1. Although organized sports at Woodview were highly competitive, informal games during the lunch period were much less competitive and tended to promote collaboration and friendship among the males.

2. Michael Messner, "When Bodies Are Weapons: Masculinity and Violence in Sport," *International Review for Sociology of Sports* 25 (1990): 207.

3. Best, *We've All Got Scars.* Also see Connell et al., *Making the Difference.*

4. Joyce Canaan, "Passing Notes and Telling Jokes: Gendered Strategies Among American Middle School Teenagers," in *Uncertain*

Terms: Negotiating Gender in American Culture, ed. Ginsburg and Lowenhaupt, 215–231.

5. Peter Lyman, "The Fraternal Bond as a Joking Relationship," in *Changing Men: New Directions in Research on Men and Masculinity,* ed. M. Kimmel (Newbury Park, Calif.: Sage, 1987), 148–163; Gregory Lehne, "Homophobia Among Men," in *The Forty-nine Percent Majority: The Male Sex Role,* ed. D. David and R. Brannon (New York: Addison-Wesley, 1976).

6. See Goffman, *Frame Analysis,* for a more extensive analysis of how storytelling allows narrators to shift frames and thereby bring out different meanings and interpretations of the events they are describing.

7. Messner, "When Bodies Are Weapons."

8. Ibid.

9. G. Fine, *With the Boys.*

10. William Labov, *Language in the Inner City: Studies in the Black English Vernacular* (Philadelphia: University of Pennsylvania Press, 1972).

11. T. Kochman, "The Boundary Between Play and Nonplay in Black Verbal Dueling," *Language in Society* 12 (1983): 329–337.

12. Lyman, "The Fraternal Bond as a Joking Relationship."

13. David Jackson, *Unmasking Masculinity: A Critical Autobiography* (London: Unwin Hyman, 1990), 177.

14. Lyman, "The Fraternal Bond as a Joking Relationship."

15. Messner, "When Bodies Are Weapons."

16. Connell et al., *Making the Difference.*

17. J. L. Dubbert, *A Man's Place: Masculinity in Transition* (Englewood-Cliffs, N.J.: Prentice-Hall, 1979); Messner, "When Bodies Are Weapons."

18. E. Dunning, "Sport As a Male Preserve: Notes on the Social Sources of Masculine Identity and its Transformations," in *Quest for Excitement: Sport and Leisure in the Civilizing Process,* ed. N. Elias and E. Dunning (New York: Basil Blackwell, 1986).

19. Connell et al., *Making the Difference;* Dunning, "Sport As a Male Preserve."

20. Messner, "When Bodies Are Weapons."

21. Ibid., 213.

22. S. Brownmiller, *Against Our Will: Men, Women, and Rape* (New York: Simon and Schuster, 1975); Dunning, "Sport as a Male Preserve."

23. Messner, When Bodies Are Weapons;" Connell et al., *Making the Difference.*

6.   *Crude Comments and Sexual Scripts*

1. Michael Messner, "Like Family: Power, Intimacy, and Sexuality in Male Athletes' Friendships," in *Men's Friendships*, ed. Peter Nardi (London: Sage, 1992), 215–237; Lyman, "The Fraternal Bond as a Joking Relationship," 148–163.

2. Messner, "Like Family"; Lyman, "The Fraternal Bond as a Joking Relationship."

3. Lyman, "The Fraternal Bond as a Joking Relationship."

4. In her research on elementary students, Thorne found that teasing exchanges could move from being playful to being irritating or malicious and then back to being playful again (*Gender Play*). She notes that the multiple layers of meaning in teasing provide opportunities to try out certain messages while keeping the option of following back on other, safer meanings.

5. Ibid.

6. It is also possible that Sam purposely used this tactic of insulting a potential girlfriend to keep Richard from gaining status within this peer group through this new relationship.

7. Lyman, "The Fraternal Bond as a Joking Relationship."

8. Messner, "Like Family."

9. In contrast to our findings and those of others regarding boys' willingness to act aggressively toward girls as well as toward other boys at school, Canaan found that boys were only aggressive toward low-status boys (and not toward girls) in her study of a predominantly middle-class school ("Passing Notes and Telling Jokes"). She attributes this to the fact that girls were considered of only marginal interest to boys in this middle school and thus primarily served as an audience for observing male insulting and joking. The disparity between the findings in her study and ours could also reflect differences resulting from social class background, with sexual harassment and insulting beginning at earlier ages in mixed-class and working-class schools than in predominantly middle-class schools.

10. Melissa Milkie, "A Social World Approach to Cultural Studies: Mass Media and Gender in the Adolescent Peer Group," *Journal of Contemporary Ethnography* 23 (1994): 354–380. This study was based on videotaped interactions of one of the low-status male peer groups in Woodview.

11. Ibid.

12. Ibid.

13. Victor Seidler, *Rediscovering Masculinity: Reason, Language, and Sexuality* (London: Routledge, 1989).

14. Maxine Baca Zinn, "Chicano Men and Masculinity," in *Men's Lives*, ed. M. Kimmel and M. Messner (New York: MacMillan, 1992), 67–77; Manuel Pena, "Class, Gender, and Maschismo," *Gender and Society* 5 (1991): 30–46.

15. Seidler, *Rediscovering Masculinity.*

16. Nan Stein, "No Laughing Matter: Sexual Harassment in K–12 Schools," in *Transforming a Rape Culture*, ed. Emile Buchwald (Minneapolis: Milkweed Editions, 1993), 313–314.

17. Ibid.

18. Ibid.

19. Chris O'Sullivan, "Fraternities and the Rape Culture," in *Transforming a Rape Culture*, ed. Buchwald, 25–30; Peggy Sanday, *Fraternity Gang Rape: Sex, Brotherhood and Privilege on Campus* (New York: New York University Press, 1992).

20. O'Sullivan, "Fraternities and the Rape Culture," 26.

21. J. Holland et al., *Pressured Pleasure: Women and the Negotiation of Sexual Boundaries* (London: Tufnell Press, 1992).

7. Learning to Smile Through the Pain

1. The fact that certain African cultures such as the Woodabe focus more on the appearance of males than females while others downplay the importance of physical beauty altogether indicates that this is a social aspect of femaleness, not a biological one. Marjorie Shostak, *NISA: The Life and Words of a Kung Woman* (New York: Random House, 1982).

2. Naomi Wolf, *The Beauty Myth* (New York: William Morrow, 1991); Sandra Lee Bartky, *Femininity and Domination* (New York: Routledge, 1990); Janet Enke, "Cultural Production, Reproduction, and Change Within an Athletic Context" (Ph.D. diss., Indiana University, 1992).

3. Enke, "Cultural Production, Reproduction, and Change."

4. Ibid.

5. Thorne, *Gender Play.*

6. Eder and Enke, "The Structure of Gossip."

7. Thorne, *Gender Play*. Thorne also found that girls referred to other girls with large breasts as "cows" when they gossiped about them. This negative evaluation of more developed girls could reflect both a fear of becoming more sexual themselves as well as jealousy toward those who were more developed than they were.

8. Eder and Enke, "The Structure of Gossip."

9. The practice of spending much of the lunch period in the bathroom was somewhat more common on the high-status side of the cafeteria, perhaps because these girls had more money to spend on makeup, blow dryers, and other beauty aids.

10. Simmons and Blyth, *Moving into Adolescence*; M. Rosenberg, "Self-Concept from Middle Childhood through Adolescence," in *Psychological Perspectives on the Self*, vol. 3, ed. J. Suls and A. Greenwald (Hillsdale, N.J.: Erlbaum, 1986), 107–136.

11. Holland and Eisenhart, *Educated in Romance*.

12. Wolf, *The Beauty Myth*.

13. Enke, "Cultural Production, Reproduction, and Change."

14. Those girls who were critical of the use of makeup may b resentful of the way in which females are expected to dissociate fron their real selves by turning their faces into masks.

15. Eder and Enke, "The Structure of Gossip."

16. Lees, *Losing Out*.

17. Evans and Eder, " 'No Exit,' " 139–170.

18. By eighth grade, most girls no longer openly ridiculed isolates. However, occasional instances such as this still took place.

19. Eckert, *Jocks and Burnouts*; Kinney, "From 'Nerds' to 'Normals.' "

20. Enke, "Cultural Production, Reproduction, and Change."

21. Arlie Hochschild, *The Managed Heart: Commercialization of Human Feeling* (Berkeley: University of California Press, 1983); Linda Valli, "Becoming Clerical Workers: Business Education and the Culture of Femininity," in *Ideology and Practice in Schooling*, ed. L. Weiss (Philadelphia: Temple University Press, 1983), 213–234.

22. Bartky, *Femininity and Domination*; Wolf, *The Beauty Myth*.

23. Wolf, *The Beauty Myth*.

24. Kathryn Morgan, "Women and the Knife: Cosmetic Surgery and the Colonization of Women's Bodies," *Hypatia* 6 (1991): 25–53.

25. Ladner, *Tomorrow's Tomorrow*.

26. Collins, *Black Feminist Thought*.

27. Kathy Davis, "Remaking the She-Devil: A Critical Look at Feminist Approaches to Beauty," *Hypatia* 6 (1991): 21–43.

28. Eder and Enke, "The Structure of Gossip."

8. *"We May Be Friends with Them, But We're Not Sluts"*

1. Simon, Eder, and Evans, "The Development of Feeling Norms Underlying Romantic Love Among Adolescent Females."

2. Ibid.

3. An alternative explanation is that these girls were not challenging heterosexuality but mocking homosexuality. Since I [Donna] did not have an opportunity to talk with them, it is unclear what they intended by these song, but the lyrics themselves challenge a heterosexual assumption within this society.

4. Michelle Fine, "Sexuality, Schooling, and Adolescent Females: The Missing Discourse of Desire," *Harvard Educational Review* 58 (1988): 29–53.

5. Simon, Eder, and Evans, "The Development of Feeling Norms Underlying Romantic Love Among Adolescent Females."

6. Lees, *Losing Out;* Valerie Walkerdine, *Schoolgirl Fictions* (New York: Verso, 1990).

7. Lees, *Sugar and Spice;* Lees, *Losing Out;* Wulff, *Twenty Girls.*

8. In another study of middle-class adolescent girls, the label *slut* was used to distinguish between girls who engaged in "kinky" sex or sex without love and girls who only had intercourse when they had determined there was a mutual sense of being in love (see Joyce Canaan, "Why a 'Slut' Is a 'Slut,'" in *Interpretative Ethnography of Education: At Home and Abroad,* ed. George Spindler and Louise Spindler [Hillsdale, N.J.: Erlbaum, 1986], 184–208). Although girls in this study reported feeling some sense of power to say yes or no to male sexual initiations, Canaan notes that the sexual encounter has already been structured with the assumption that boys have sexual desires and girls do not.

9. While traditional views of sexuality are being mocked, Andrea still takes on the role of being a prostitute to do so. Thus, these girls only achieve a level of deflection rather than challenging the label itself.

10. Lees, *Sugar and Spice.*

11. M. Fine, "Sexuality, Schooling, and Adolescent Females."

12. Lees, *Sugar and Spice.*

13. McRobbie, "Working Class Girls and the Culture of Femininity," 96–108; Kessler et al., "Gender Relations in Secondary Schooling," 34–47.

14. Also, when the teasing comments shifted from Annie's relationship to a popular novel, it may have made it easier for Annie to begin to detach and join in on the collective humor.

15. McRobbie, "Working Class Girls and the Culture of Femininity."

16. M. Fine, "Sexuality, Schooling, and Adolescent Females," 29–53.

17. Audre Lorde, *Sister Outsider* (Freedom, Calif.: The Crossing Press, 1984).

18. M. Weinberg, R. Swenson, and S. Hammersmith, "Sexual Autonomy and the Status of Women," *Social Problems* 30 (1983): 312–324.

19. Lorde, *Sister Outsider.*

20. Alice Walker, *You Can't Keep a Good Woman Down* (New York: Harcourt Brace Jovanovich, 1982).

9. Reconsidering Gender, Talk, and Inequality

1. David Maltz and Ruth Barker, "A Cultural Approach to Male-Female Miscommunication," in *Language and Social Identity*, ed. John Gumperz (New York: Cambridge University Press, 1983), 105–216; Tannen, *You Just Don't Understand.*

2. Lois Banner, *American Beauty* (Chicago: University of Chicago Press, 1983).

3. Wolf, *The Beauty Myth.*

4. Banner, *American Beauty;* Morgan, "Women and the Knife."

5. Davis, "Remaking the She-Devil."

6. Ibid.

7. Bartky, *Femininity and Domination.*

8. Weinberg, Swenson, and Hammersmith, "Sexual Autonomy and the Status of Women."

9. Christine Overall, "What's Wrong with Prostitution?: Evaluating Sex Work," *Signs* 17 (1992): 705–724.

10. Lori Sudderth, "Victim or Survivor?: The Sociological Context of Coping with Sexual Assault" (Ph.D. diss., Indiana University, 1993).

11. Valerie Walkerdine, "Girlhood Through the Looking Glass" (Paper presented at Alice in Wonderland: First International Conference on Girls and Girlhood, Amsterdam, The Netherlands, 1992).

12. Lorde, *Sister Outsider.*

13. Bartky, *Femininity and Domination.*

14. Seidler, *Rediscovering Masculinity.*

15. Ibid.

16. Clyde Franklin, "Hey, Home—Yo, Bro: Friendships Among Black Men," in *Men's Friendships*, ed. Nardi, 201–214.

10. *Where Do We Go from Here?*

1. Messner, "When Bodies are Weapons," 203–217.

2. Dunning, "Sport as a Male Preserve."

3. Ibid.

4. According to Enke, high school female basketball players and other athletes often feel pressure to look attractive as well as to perform well. This is due less to the actual athletic events than to the focus on appearance elsewhere in their schools and in society at large, however ("Cultural Production, Reproduction, and Change").

5. Paula Gunn Allen, "I Climb the Mesas in my Dreams," in *Survival This Way*, ed. Joseph Bruchac (Tucson: University of Arizona Press, 1987), 1–21.

6. Collins, *Black Feminist Thought.*

7. Carby, "It Jus Be's Dat Way Sometime."

8. Stein, "No Laughing Matter."

9. For a comprehensive debate on the degree to which differences exist between boys and girls see Thorne, *Gender Play.*

10. Ibid.

11. Goodman, *Elementary Schooling for Critical Democracy.*
12. Ibid.
13. A related strategy would be to say, "Could you repeat that please. I'd like to get it in my notes." In one seminar where I [Donna] brought up these suggestions, it was agreed that sociological jargon can be pretty deadly, so it might as well be used when trying to confront particularly harmful aspects of peer culture.

Appendix.   Notes on Methodology

1. Some of the ethnographies that have used multiple researchers include Connell et al., *Making the Difference;* Thorne, *Gender Play;* and Adler, Kless, and Adler, "Socialization to Gender Roles." Studies that have relied more extensively on interviewing students have been more successful at studying a wider range of groups (for example, Schofield, *Black and White in School;* Eckert, *Jocks and Burnouts;* Kinney, "From 'Nerds' to 'Normals' "). These studies, however, often lack the detailed information about students' naturally occurring activities that can best be obtained through observation and/or tape-recorded conversations.

2. In three cases, the researcher had left the group to study another group before we introduced tape recorders into the setting. In two other groups, the routine speech activities studied here were less common, in one case because the group consisted of only two members and in another case because the group was made up primarily of special education students who, primarily due to their wide range of social and communication skill levels, tended not to engage in these routines with each other.

3. Throughout the book we present examples of each activity from our field notes and from the tape-recorded conversations. This allows readers to decide for themselves whether the students modified their routine behaviors during tape-recorded interactions.

4. I [Donna] have also helped develop a student club called KACTIS (Kids Against Cruel Treatment in School) to help students become better prepared to deal with peer conflict and ridicule. This club is discussed in more detail in the last chapter. See also Evans and Eder, " 'No Exit.' "

Selected Bibliography

Adler, Patricia, Steven Kless, and Peter Adler. 1992. "Socialization to Gender Roles: Elementary School Boys and Girls." *Sociology of Education* 65: 169–187.

Canaan, Joyce. 1987. "A Comparative Analysis of American Suburban Middle Class, Middle School, and High School Teenage Culture." In George Spindler and Louise Spinler, eds., *Interpretative Ethnography of Education: At Home and Abroad*. Hillsdale, N.J.: Lawrence Erlbaum Associates.

Connell, Robert. 1987. *Gender and Power*. Stanford: Stanford University Press.

Connell, R., D. Ashenden, S. Kessler, and G. Dowsett. 1982. *Making the Difference: Schools, Families, and Social Division*. Sydney: Allen and Unwin.

Corsaro, William. 1985. *Friendship and Peer Culture in the Early Years*. Norwood, N.J.: Ablex.

————. 1992. "Interpretive Reproduction in Children's Peer Cultures." *Social Psychology Quarterly* 55:160–177.

Corsaro, William, and Donna Eder. 1990. "Children's Peer Cultures." *Annual Review of Sociology* 16:197–220.

————. 1994. "The Development and Socialization of Children and Adolescents." In K. Cook, G. Fine, and J. House, eds., *Sociological Perspectives on Social Psychology*. New York: Allyn and Bacon.

Coward, R., and J. Ellis. 1977. *Language and Materialism: Developments in Semiology and the Theory of the Subject*. London: Routledge and Kegan Paul.

Davis, Kathy. 1991. "Remaking the She-Devil: A Critical Look at Feminist Approaches to Beauty." *Hypatia* 6:21–43.

Eckert, Penelope. 1989. *Jocks and Burnouts: Social Categories and Identity in the High School*. New York: Teachers College Press.

Eder, D. 1985. "The Cycle of Popularity: Interpersonal Relations Among Female Adolescents." *Sociology of Education* 58:154–165.

————. 1991. "The Role of Teasing in Adolescent Peer Culture." In S. Cahill, ed., *Sociological Studies of Child Development*, vol. 4. Greenwich, Conn.: JAI Press.

Eder, D., and J. Enke. 1991. "The Structure of Gossip: Opportunities and Constraints on Collective Expression Among Adolescents." *American Sociological Review* 56:495–508.

Eder, D., and S. Parker. 1987. "The Cultural Production and Reproduction of Gender: The Effect of Extracurricular Activities on Peer Group Culture." *Sociology of Education* 60:200–213.

Enke, Janet. 1992. "Cultural Production, Reproduction, and Change Within an Athletic Context." Ph.D. diss., Indiana University.

Evans, Cathy, and Donna Eder. 1993. " 'No Exit': Processes of Social Isolation in the Middle School." *Journal of Contemporary Ethnography* 22:139–170.

Fine, Gary. 1987. *With the Boys: Little League Baseball and Preadolescent Culture*. Chicago: University of Chicago Press.

Fine, Michelle. 1988. "Sexuality, Schooling, and Adolescent Females: The Missing Discourse of Desire." *Harvard Educational Review*. 58:29–53.

Fisher, Sue, and Alexandra Todd. 1986. *Discourse and Institutional Authority: Medicine, Education and Law*. Norwood, N.J.: Ablex.

Goodman, Jesse. 1992. *Elementary Schooling for Critical Democracy*. Albany: State University of New York Press.

Goodwin, Marjorie. 1990. *He-Said-She-Said: Talk as Social Organization among Black Children*. Bloomington: Indiana University Press.

Griffin, Christine. 1985. *Typical Girls?: Young Women from School to the Job Market*. London: Routledge.

Holland, Dorothy, and Margaret Eisenhart. 1990. *Educated in Romance: Women, Achievement, and College Culture*. Chicago: University of Chicago Press.

Kessler, S., D. Ashenden, R. Connell, and G. Dowsett. 1985. "Gender Relations in Secondary Schooling." *Sociology of Education* 58:34–47.

Kinney, David. 1990. "Dweebs, Headbangers, and Trendies: Adolescent Identity Formation and Change within Socio-Cultural Contexts." Ph.D. diss., Indiana University.

———. 1993. "From 'Nerds' to 'Normals': Adolescent Identity Recovery within a Changing School Social System." *Sociology of Education* 66:21–40.

Lees, Sue. 1986. *Losing Out: Sexuality and Adolescent Girls*. London: Hutchinson.

———. 1993. *Sugar and Spice*. London: Hutchinson.

Lorde, Audre. 1984. *Sister Outsider*. Freedom, Calif.: The Crossing Press.

Lyman, Peter. 1987. "The Fraternal Bond as a Joking Relationship." In M. Kimmel, ed., *Changing Men: New Directions in Research on Men and Masculinity*. Newbury Park, Calif.: Sage.

Messner, Michael. 1990. "When Bodies Are Weapons: Masculinity and Violence in Sport." *International Review for Sociology of Sports* 25:203–217.

———. 1992. "Like Family: Power, Intimacy, and Sexuality in Male Athletes' Friendships." In Peter Nardi, ed., *Men's Friendships*. London: Sage.

Parker, Stephen. 1991. "Early Adolescent Male Cultures: The Importance of Organized and Informal Sport." Ph.D. diss. Indiana University.

Pena, Manuel. 1991. "Class, Gender, and Maschismo." *Gender and Society* 5:30–46.

Schofield, Janet. 1982. *Black and White in School*. New York: Praeger.
Seidler, Victor. 1989. *Rediscovering Masculinity: Reason, Language, and Sexuality*. London: Routledge.
Simmons, Roberta, and Dale Blyth. 1987. *Moving into Adolescence: The Impact of Pubertal Change and School Context*. New York: Aldine de Gruyter.
Simon, Robin, Donna Eder, and Cathy Evans. 1992. "The Development of Feeling Norms Underlying Romantic Love Among Adolescent Females." *Social Psychology Quarterly* 55:29–46.

Tannen, Deborah. 1990. *You Just Don't Understand: Women and Men in Conversation*. New York: William Morrow.
Thorne, Barrie. 1993. *Gender Play: Boys and Girls in School*. New Brunswick, N.J.: Rutgers University Press.
Thorne, Barrie, and Zella Luria. 1986. "Sexuality and Gender in Children's Daily Worlds." *Social Problems* 33:176–189.
Todd, Alexandra Dundas, and Sue Fisher. 1988. "Theories of Gender, Theories of Discourse." In A. Todd and S. Fisher, eds., *Gender and Discourse: The Power of Talk*. Norwood, N.J.: Ablex.

Walkerdine, Valerie. 1990. *Schoolgirl Fictions*. New York: Verso.
Willis, Paul. 1981. *Learning to Labour*. New York: Columbia University Press.
Wolf, Naomi. 1991. *The Beauty Myth*. New York: William Morrow.
Wulff, Helena. 1988. *Twenty Girls: Growing Up, Ethnicity and Excitement in a South London Microculture*. Stockholm Studies in Social Anthropology, no. 21. Stockholm, Sweden: University of Stockholm.

Index

abuse, 152, 164; physical, 15, 77, 175; sexual, 4–6, 77, 89, 153. *See also* verbal abuse
academic achievement, 13, 14, 26, 27
acceptance, peer, 17, 20–21, 48, 50, 54, 56–58; in smaller schools, 156–157, 164–165
acquaintance rape, 4–5, 77, 146
advice columns, in teen magazines, 146
Afro-Americans, 8–9, 12–14, 46–48, 55–56, 121, 178n8; ritual insulting among, 17, 182n48
aggression/aggressiveness, male, 6, 18, 45, 61–72, 78–81, 154; Canaan's findings, 187n9; in lunchroom interactions, 27; researchers' perspectives on, 174; seen as traditional masculine behavior, 15, 64, 157–158. *See also* competition/

competitiveness; fighting, physical; sexual aggression
aggression, use by female isolates, 54
Allen, Paula Gunn, 160
alternative schools, 56–57, 164–165, 167
anger, 86–89, 100, 102, 133–136, 168
anorexia, 114, 153
appearance: female, 5, 14, 91, 111–112, 120–123, 148; control factors, 113–118; focus on in girls, 37, 103–108, 129, 160; girls' criticisms of male, 108; girls' gossip about, 28, 109–118, 122–123; insults about, 118–120; media messages on, 118, 151, 160; in non-Western cultures, 188n1; role in objectification of females, 151–153, 162; role in seeing student as deviant, 40; and standards of beauty,

INDEX

sexuality (*continued*)
teasing about, 86–91, 143–145. *See also* double standard
sexuality, female, 15–16, 114, 116–118, 132, 146–148, 152; challenging messages on, 100–101; negative labeling of, 11, 15, 128–136, 153, 162, 179n17, 190nn8, 9; teasing about, 139–146
sexuality, male, 96–99, 100–101, 147–148, 152–153, 155, 164
sexual objects, females viewed as, 96–98, 118, 123, 141–142, 152–153, 162; by adolescent boys, 16, 85–86, 88–90, 98–102, 128–130, 151
"sissy," as label, 150, 155
sixth-graders, 23–24, 32, 55, 183n8. *See also* boys; girls
"slag," as label, 11, 15, 132, 179n17
"slut," as label, 10, 11, 15, 150, 153, 162; behavior believed calling for, 5, 129–133, 135, 190n8; double standard demonstrated by, 133; responses to, 133–135
smiling, while cheerleading, 104–106
snobbishness, 38–39, 41–45, 57, 122
soccer, 64, 158
social change, 7, 151–153, 157–161
social inequality, relationship to gender inequality, 157–158. *See also* hierarchies/y; status, social
social interaction, 4, 7–8, 10–12, 23–25, 56; audio- and video-taping by researchers, 172–175, 193n3; between researchers and students, 22; social ranking reinforced within, 40–41. *See also* routines
socialization, 32–33, 147–148
social ranking, *see* hierarchies/y, social; status, social
society, 55, 58, 61, 147, 157–161; racism in, 46, 48
"sociobabble" (sociological jargon), as response to verbal abuse, 169–170, 193n11
sophistication, sexual, appearance of, 136–139

special education students, 21, 26, 28–29, 53–54, 56, 193n2; abuse of, 76–77, 77, 119–120; as candidates for social isolation, 49–50
speech, 1, 2, 4, 10, 28–29, 149. *See also* language; routines
Spender, Dale, 11
sports, *see* athletics
Spur Posse Gang case, 5, 6
status, social, 12–14, 26–29, 155, 159–160, 171, 182n5; addressing problems of, 166–167; differing perspectives on, 36–40, 57, 182n5; enhancement through insulting, 73–76, 79; insecurity about, 54, 58; relationship to popularity, 31–36; relationship to race, 16, 46–48, 55–56; relationship to social class, 40–46; role of aggressiveness in, 69, 84–85. *See also* hierarchies/y; high-status students; low-status students
Stein, Nan, 101–102
storytelling, 17, 22, 27–28, 102, 137–139, 186n6; by boys, 64–67, 71–72, 91, 96–99; collaborative, 10, 78, 137–139, 150
subcultures, 9, 121, 132
suicide, of isolates, 51
swearing, 22, 174

talk, *see* collaborative talk; speech
Tannen, Deborah, 9
tape recording, use in research, 172–175, 193nn2, 3
team approach to data collection, 21–24, 171–175, 193n1
teasing, 2–3, 10, 22, 28–29, 127, 150–151, 187n4; collaborative, 17, 139–146, 191n14; confronting and controlling, 57, 141, 168–169; gender messages in, 12, 17; sexual, 86–95, 91, 93–95, 100; about snobbishness, 44–45
territory, *see* seating patterns
Thorne, Barrie, 15, 108, 166, 183n8, 189n7, 193n1; on sexual teasing, 88–89, 187n4
Todd, Alexandra, 11–12

About the Authors

Donna Eder is Professor of Sociology at Indiana University. She has published widely on many aspects of peer culture, gender and discourse, and school life. Among other things she is currently doing research on conflict resolution in schools.

Catherine Colleen Evans is Director of the John Rivers Communication Museum at the College of Charleston. She has worked as an adolescent counselor and social worker and is currently completing *Yesterday's Songs: The Adolescent Diaries of Three Contemporary Women*.

Stephen Parker is Assistant Professor of Sociology at the University of Montevallo. He has published articles in a variety of sociology journals.